CHATHAM HOUSE PAPERS

Britain, Germany and 1992

The Limits of Deregulation

**Stephen Woolcock,
Michael Hodges and
Kristin Schreiber**

The Royal Institute of International Affairs

Pinter Publishers
London

© Royal Institute of International Affairs, 1991

First published in Great Britain in 1991 by
Pinter Publishers Limited
25 Floral Street, London WC2E 9DS

British Library Cataloguing in Publication Data

A CIP catalogue record of this book is available from the British Library

ISBN 0-86187-172-3 (Paperback)
    0-86187-171-5 (Hardback)

Reproduced from copy supplied by
Koinonia Limited
Printed and bound in Great Britain by
Biddles Ltd

CONTENTS

CHATHAM HOUSE PAPERS

A West European Programme Publication
Programme Director: Helen Wallace

The Royal Institute of International Affairs, at Chatham House in London, has provided an impartial forum for discussion and debate on current international issues for some 70 years. Its resident research fellows, specialized information resources, and range of publications, conferences, and meetings span the fields of international politics, economics, and security. The Institute is independent of government.

Chatham House Papers are short monographs on current policy problems which have been commissioned by the RIIA. In preparing the papers, authors are advised by a study group of experts convened by the RIIA, and publication of a paper indicates that the Institute regards it as an authoritative contribution to the public debate. The Institute does not, however, hold opinions of its own; the views expressed in this publication are the responsibility of the authors.

ABBREVIATIONS

ABB	ASEA Brown-Boveri
AFNOR	Association Française de Normalisation
AT&T	American Telephone and Telegraph
BAV	Bundesaufsichtsamt für das Versicherungswesen
BDA	Bundesvereinigung der Deutschen Arbeitgeberverbände
BDI	Bundesverband der Deutschen Industrie
BSI	British Standards Institute
BT	British Telecom
CCITT	Consultative Committee on International Telex and Tele-communications
CDU	Christian Democratic Union
CEA	European Association of Insurers
CEN	European Committee for Standardization
CENELEC	European Committee for the Coordination of Electrical Standards
CEPT	European Conference of Post & Telecommunications Authorities
CGE	Compagnie Générale d'Electricité
CSU	Christian Social Union
DBP	Deutsche Bundespost
DGB	Deutscher Gewerkschaftsbund (German Federation of Trade Unions)
DIN	Deutsche Industrie-Normen (German Industry Standards)
DKE	Deutsche Kommission für Elektrotechnik
ECISS	European Committee for Iron and Steel Standardization (part of CEN)
ECJ	European Court of Justice
EDF	Electricité de France

EN	European Standard
ETSI	European Telecommunications Standards Institute
EUTELSAT	European Telecommunications Satellite Organization
FCC	Federal Communications Commission
FSA	Financial Services Act
GDV	Association of German Insurers
GEC	General Electricity Company
GPT	GEC Plessey Telecommunications
ICA	Insurance Companies Act
IEC	International Electrotechnical Committee
ISO	International Standards Organization
ITT	International Telephone and Telegraph Corporation
ITU	International Telecommunications Union
LVD	Low Voltage Directive
MMC	Monopolies and Mergers Commission
NEDC	National Economic Development Council
NEDO	National Economic Development Office
OFT	Office of Fair Trading
ONP	Open Network Provision
OSO	Offshore Supplies Office
PTO	Public Telecommunication Organization
PTT	Postes, Télégraphes et Téléphones
RACE	Research & Development in Advanced Communications Technologies for Europe
RAS	Reunione Adriatica di Ficurtá
RPB	Recognized Professional Body
RWE	Rheinland-Westfälisches Elektrizitätswerke
SBCD	Second Banking Coordination Directive
SEA	Single European Act (1985)
SEL	Standard Elektrik Lorenz
SIB	Securities and Investment Board
SRO	Self-regulating Organization
TUC	Trades Union Congress
TüV	Technische Überwachungsvereine
UNI	Italian Standards Institution
UNICE	Union of Industries of the European Community
UTE	Union Technique de l'Electricité
VAG	Versicherungsaufsichtsgesetz
VDMA	German Machinery and Equipment Manufacturers
VVG	Versicherungsvertraggesetz

PREFACE

The purpose of the research project on which this volume is based was to address three key questions: Will a single market be realized? What will it look like? And what impact will it have on national approaches to market regulation and vice versa?

The study has been undertaken jointly by the West European Programme at the Royal Institute of International Affairs in London and the Institut für Europäische Politik in Bonn. The research was carried out by staff at the two institutes and funded by the Anglo-German Foundation for the Study of the Industrial Society.

The project team examined six case-studies: mergers and acquisitions; public procurement; technical standards; telecommunications; banking; and insurance. These were chosen because they account for some 60% of the potential gains to be derived from the creation of a single market as estimated in the 'cost of non-Europe' study that accompanied the Cecchini Report in 1988. They also cover areas in which the single market will have a significant impact on the regulatory regimes, and thus the competitive environment, within which companies will in the future have to operate.

The focus on Britain and Germany permits a comparison of two contrasting approaches to 1992. The British government's approach is characterized by a determination to ensure that the 1992 process does not reverse the Anglo-American deregulation revolution of 1980s; Germany is equally determined to defend the national social consensus (rooted in a process of consultation between government, employers and unions) on which the Germans believe that their prosperity has been based.

In order to examine the interaction between market-led and policy-led forces, each case-study focused on an analysis of a key area of EC legislation. These were the merger-control regulation, the excluded-sectors (or utilities) directive in public procurement in financial services, the new-approach directives in technical standards, the second banking coordination directive and the second insurance directive. In each case, related pieces of legislation were also covered, such as legislation affecting takeovers or the compliance/remedies directives in public procurement. In total some 150 interviews were carried out in Britain and Germany with industrialists, trade associations, trade unionists and government officials. Some further interviews were carried out in Brussels and France. Although much of the analysis of market factors and the emerging shape of EC legislation is valid for the EC as a whole, the concentration of interviews in Britain and Germany means that our conclusions do not necessarily apply to other member-states.

The case-studies fall into two broad categories: the 'horizontal' issues, discussed in Chapters 2-4, of mergers, standards and public procurement; and the sectoral case-studies, in Chapters 5 and 6, covering telecommunications, banking and insurance. All the studies interlink – procurement and standards issues are, for example, of central importance to telecommunications, and the liberalization of telecommunications services is not without relevance to cross-border trade in financial services. The study concludes with a comparative analysis of the interaction between the EC's single market programme and the two national approaches of Britain and Germany.

We would like to thank the Anglo-German Foundation for the Study of Industrial Society for funding both the research work and a conference in Bonn in March 1990, as well as providing publication expenses. The project was immensely strengthened by the active support and cooperation of experts and practitioners from business and government, who gave generously of their time and advice, both individually and in study groups. We are also grateful to all those people in Britain, Germany, the European Commission and elsewhere who agreed to be interviewed by researchers. The views expressed in this volume are, of course, those of the researchers. Finally, we would like to thank the staff at both institutes, and in particular Dorothee Kempf, Nicolette McCormick, Clare Pyatt, Zoë Harris and Alex Bellinger, as well as Hannah Doe for her efficient management of the publication process.

February 1991   Helen Wallace
                                                        Wolfgang Wessels

1

REVIEW OF FINDINGS

By June 1988, the date of the Rhodes summit, the European Community's member-states had come to the conclusion that their initiative to create a single European market by the end of 1992 had gathered such momentum that the process was now irreversible. That they had reached this conclusion is all the more remarkable in that few people had any clear idea what a single market would look like when it did materialize. Some saw the 1992 phenomenon as consisting more of rhetoric than of substance; others considered that market-led developments were bringing about a single market almost regardless of what might happen on the legislative front.[1]

In some areas, such as fiscal approximation or border controls, there were few signs of progress towards the objectives of the European Commission's 1985 White Paper.[2] In others, such as technical standards or public procurement, non-statutory barriers to market entry would clearly persist even when there was agreement on legislation.[3] As for what the single market would look like, some saw it as the greatest exercise in deregulation ever undertaken, while others regarded it as an opportunity to replace conflicting or non-existent national regulation with a coherent and consistent system of regulation at the Community level. Business leaders welcomed the prospect of a single market free of the rigidities caused by national regulation; unions were concerned about social dumping in which the high standards of safety or social provisions achieved in some countries would be undermined. Others saw this not as a danger but as a positive extension of the process of deregulation.[4]

That the single market meant all things to all people no doubt contri-

1

buted to the success of the 1992 concept, enhancing its role as a catalyst for change. But what will really change? Will a genuine single market be achieved in which a producer of goods or services will really be able to supply customers throughout the EC from its home base? Or will certain barriers, whether statutory or non-statutory, remain? Will the 1992 process create a deregulatory chain reaction and sweep all barriers before it, and in so doing undermine established levels of customer protection and social standards? Or will 1992 result in the reregulation of markets at an EC level? What impact will it have on the member-states? Does the 1992 'competition among rules' approach to integration mean that the economically weaker member-states, such as Britain, will be obliged to adopt the rules of the more successful countries, such as Germany?

Three main issues are addressed in this study: the extent to which a single European market will actually be achieved; the characteristics of this market, in particular whether 1992 will result in deregulation or reregulation; and the interaction of the single market and national regulatory policies. Furthermore, it examines whether the Community approach to market regulation will be closer to the 'deregulatory' British or the more 'consensual' German model. The answers to these questions will have a direct bearing on everyone touched by the integration of markets in Europe, whether employer or employee, producer or customer, manufacturer or service provider. They will, of course, also have a bearing on the EC's trading partners and neighbours. More indirectly, but equally importantly, they will affect the scope for future integration within the EC. Finally, if 1992 represents a 'new approach' to the regulation of integrating markets, the lessons learnt in Europe may be of relevance to the wider debate on how to deal with the progressive integration of global markets.

Will the single market be achieved?

Research on the core elements of the 1992 programme has shown that a combination of market-led and policy-led factors has brought about changes in the practice and behaviour of companies and trade unions that make a single market possible, even in sectors where there are entrenched non-statutory barriers to trade. Although there is little doubt that a single market will be achieved, it will certainly not be one devoid of local-market characteristics. Many of these will remain, as will the need, in a number of cases, to have local-market presence in order to gain effective market access.

2

It is important to remember that the 1985 White Paper outlining the steps towards a single European market was not a pioneering initiative; the Community has had the aim of becoming a common market since it was first conceived. Over the three decades since then, treaties and secondary legislation have removed most of the statutory barriers in the EC, so that in many sectors – especially those in which consumer-orientated products predominate – a single market already exists. But in a number of areas the non-statutory barriers, and those represented by the national regulatory policies, are still in full operation. Some of these barriers are formidable, and the case-studies outlined in the following chapters illustrate why they have remained intact despite numerous attempts to eliminate them.

The driving forces behind the EC's 1992 programme fall into two broad categories: market-led and policy-led. Predominant among market-led factors has been the impact of global competition and technology. The progressive globalization of business has made it impossible for companies heavily dependent on national markets to remain internationally competitive – largely because increased technological sophistication means that the economies of scale needed to fund product development can no longer be achieved in purely national markets. Despite these pressures, entrenched national thinking and practices have meant that few of the old national champions have ventured willingly beyond their home territory, as the case-studies in telecommunications and public purchasing show. Instead they have been pushed into it by a competitor 'breaking ranks' from the established – often oligopolistic – market structures in order to gain a competitive edge by establishing a presence across the whole European market. But such market-led forces would not by themselves have generated the same momentum that 1992 did. Many business people interviewed for this study said that 1992 had caused them to bring forward decisions that they would have made in due course. There is none the less clear evidence in a number of case-studies that the degree of market integration now taking place would not have been as significant without the introduction as well of policy-led forces.

Predominant among policy-led factors has been the application of 'competition among rules', based on the principles of mutual recognition of standards and home-country regulatory control in financial services, which has created a form of deregulatory dynamic. Thus, if companies from country 'A' can utilize liberal rules applying in their home country to compete in the market of country 'B', country 'B' has little to gain by blocking common EC rules and retaining tighter national regulations,

3

which will merely have the effect of penalizing its own companies; indeed, common EC rules may be the only way to contain the pressure for deregulation from country 'A'. One of the hypotheses that we set out to test was that this form of competition among rules would result in competitive deregulation. If successful companies are those that steal a march on their competitors by anticipating the single market, is there a parallel in national regulatory policy, and, if so, has such national deregulation set off a deregulatory chain reaction?

It is clear that policy decisions in each of the major EC institutions contribute towards a deregulatory dynamic. Since majority voting operates for measures covered by the Commission's 1985 White Paper (with the exception of fiscal approximation and dismantling border controls), one or two member-states cannot block EC directives. There is therefore an incentive to compromise.

The two institutions that have played a vital and active role in bringing about the single market are the European Court of Justice (ECJ) and the European Commission. The former has had a direct impact on the process of market integration. Its decisions have influenced the shape of EC regulation directly through interpretation of the treaties and secondary EC legislation, and it fulfils a vital role in the enforcement of the directives already agreed. It has also played a key role by forcing the hands of member-states on issues that they have been seeking to avoid: the new approach to technical harmonization and standards-making, for example, derives from the Court's judgment in the *Cassis de Dijon* case.[5]

The European Commission is, of course, the initiator of new policy proposals. Since 1985 it has adopted a pragmatic approach, maintaining the momentum of the 1992 process by basing decisions more frequently on competition among rules rather than holding out for agreement on a perfect 'European' solution.

Finally, there has been external political pressure. In some cases this has helped reluctant member-states to liberalize. For example, US pressure on the Federal Republic of Germany to liberalize its telecommunications regime played a key role in overcoming national resistance to change. Outside pressure has also had an impact on the shape of EC directives: thus the reciprocity provisions of the Second Banking Coordination Directive (SBCD) were influenced by US and Japanese views.

What will the single market be like?
Although the evidence gathered here indicates that 1992 will almost certainly result in the erosion of national regulatory regimes, the case-studies also show that there are limits to competitive deregulation. Every regulatory regime or set of standards represents a form of national social contract that reflects a particular domestic consensus or balance between competing interests. There are clear differences of view over what regulations are really necessary, and, in addition, protectionist motives are often present. But, whatever form national regimes take, individual governments are generally reluctant to see them eroded by EC proposals.

If national regulation is removed, one solution to the need for some form of regime would be the introduction of agreed common minimum requirements controlled at EC level, i.e. reregulation. This raises questions concerning the type and extent of such EC-level regulation and where to draw the line between national and EC competence, since each member-state has its regulatory sacred cows over which it will fight to retain control.

Indeed one of the main findings of this study is that often member-states simply have not been able to agree on the objectives to be pursued by such new EC-level regulatory powers and therefore only a limited degree of discretionary power to regulate is being transferred to the EC level. In this sense the 1992 process is deregulatory, in that it is leading to the establishment of a European framework of rules which limits the ability of national regulators to intervene but does not introduce extensive discretionary powers at the EC level to counteract these limitations.

The persistence of non-statutory barriers makes some EC regulation necessary if liberalization is to be achieved and the objective of both creating and maintaining a genuine single market be fulfilled. But, although it is increasingly recognized that there is a strong case for the EC to be granted discretionary powers for this purpose, member-states are in practice reluctant to allow it to use these powers to force through liberalization. For example, in the telecommunications sector, four national governments have resorted to the ECJ in an effort to block the Commission's efforts to implement Article 90 (EEC), rather than Article 100a (EEC), as a means of challenging the restrictive practices anchored in the national regulatory regimes.

Despite this apparent resistance to reregulation, in sectors in which the old national regulatory regimes have become counter-productive,

5

national regulators have begun to look to EC-wide measures to re-establish regulatory control. In the case of the natural monopolies, such as telecommunications, energy and transport, there is a need to anchor national regulations in a European framework to defend them against any undermining by global competition, although some would like to see more competition introduced in these sectors. Since the EC does not have the power to force liberalization, it is in the interests of the national monopolies to push for reregulation.

The impact of 1992 on national approaches to regulation

The current liberal economic policies of the German and British governments broadly coincide, but their approaches to the single market differ as a result of the underlying differences in their respective attitudes to regulation. What impact will the creation of a single market have on these different approaches? What do our case-studies tell us about how the economic architecture of each state is adjusting to the emerging EC superstructure? Will the 'competition-among-rules' approach of the single market result in convergence? Which of the various types of rules or national approaches to market regulation will prove the more influential? In the context of our Anglo-German comparison, will the economic power of Germany, possibly further strengthened by German unification, ensure that the German approach prevails, or will the British free-market approach ultimately prove irresistible?

In order to answer these questions it is helpful to assess the differences between the two countries in terms of the following: the fundamental approaches to the role of the state in the economy, or what might be called the architecture of the state; the general scale of regulation in the economy; and the extent to which regulatory decisions are based on corporatist structures of consultation and consensus.

Germany, like most of continental Western Europe, has a tradition of public administrative law that finds expression in its approach to market regulation. It has a number of consistent regulatory regimes, which generally have a statutory base, pursue long-term policy objectives and are established after wide consultation with the social partners and interest groups. These regimes, which are known collectively as '*Ordnungspolitik*', limit day-to-day political or discretionary intervention by government. Where fine-tuning of decisions is required, this is generally entrusted to independent regulatory bodies that are accountable to parliament, but also partially insulated from political control through the public law that governs their operations. The best known example of this approach is, of course, the Bundesbank, which, although obliged to support government economic policy objectives, carries out monetary policy independently of day-to-day political interference from government.

In contrast, the traditional British approach is based on the interpretation of public interest by the government of the day. The absence of public law, of German-type economic elements in the constitution, or even of a broad consensus, leaves the government of the day with much greater discretionary power. Regulatory policies are translated into statutes and therefore achieve a form of consistency, but they remain susceptible to a short-term change in policy or a change of government. As the debate about sovereignty and the EC shows, the British see the Palace of Westminster as providing its essential architecture of the state.

During the 1980s, both Germany and Britain could be classified as EC members that actively pursued market-oriented policies. In the British case, however, three successive Conservative governments have introduced radical deregulation and privatization policies that have significantly reduced the role of the state in the economy. Although Britain started the decade with a higher level of regulation than in Germany, by the end of it the role of the state in the economy was much less than in Germany. At present there is probably more public ownership in Germany, and, although it is still too early to say what effects unification will have, it seems likely that the important sectors will continue to be publicly owned. Unification could also result in an increase rather than a decrease in market regulation as the social market economy is extended.

The scale of regulatory intervention also varies between sectors of the economy. A range of historical and political factors has produced varying patterns of market regulation in particular sectors. Although Germany has a relatively liberal economy compared with the rest of the EC, in several sectors there are entrenched regulatory practices. These constitute the sacred cows that even liberal-minded German politicians and businessmen are reluctant to sacrifice for 1992. When such sacred cows are slaughtered, the political heat that is generated could give the impression that 1992 is bringing about 'revolutionary' change. Yet, however important such change is for the sector concerned, it must be seen in the context of the economy as a whole. By contrast, during the 1980s the British had become accustomed to so much domestically generated change that the deregulatory nature of the 1992 process seldom ran up against major resistance on detail.

One of the most striking differences between the two countries is the virtual absence in Britain of any effort to establish a consensus, whereas in Germany consensus and consultation are of central importance. In Britain's case voluntarism has become the accepted norm. But in Germany patterns of consultation are often embedded in statutes, and it is expected that political parties, social partners and interest groups should be engaged in a continuous dialogue.

In the 1980s, practices diverged rather than converged. Under the influence of successive Conservative governments, the British have moved away from anything approaching a social contract, whether implicit or explicit, and there has been a growth in the relative power of central government. The Germans, by contrast, have retained their commitment to explicit or implicit social contracts at national, sectoral and company levels, the political desirability of which is endorsed by all parties. Therefore the ability of the Federal government to dictate policy is limited. These contrasting approaches are illustrated by the way in which liberalization of telecommunications was pursued in the two countries. In Britain, ministers decided the structure of the sector; in Germany there was detailed consultation with business, unions, consumers, Länder authorities and so on, with considerable efforts being made to reach a consensus (see Chapter 5).

These different national approaches have found expression in the responses of each country to 1992. In Germany, the Federal government held a series of 'Europe conferences' (*Nationale Europa Konferenzen*) for a very wide range of interest groups in order to foster a national consensus on the key issues. Employers and unions, in the shape of the BDI, BDA and DGB, held joint meetings and issued joint communiqués. In contrast, the only British attempt at tripartite consultation on 1992 took the form of a few meetings held by the – considerably weakened – National Economic Development Council (NEDC). The British response was not to strengthen channels of consultation but to mount public information campaigns. Both the Department of Trade and Industry (DTI) and the Confederation of British Industry (CBI) conducted extensive and successful campaigns aimed at bringing home the importance of the 1992 programme to as many companies as possible. From an early stage, there was concern among officials in the DTI that British business would not make the most of the opportunities offered by 1992. But in general, neither the DTI nor the CBI sought to develop and enhance consultation, i.e., a flow of information back from companies and other interest groups, on what they wanted from EC regulation. The CBI even

8

separated its 1992 initiative from its mainstream committee consultation structure, thus ensuring that information flowed only one way.

Although this volume does not address the social dimension as such, each piece of 1992 legislation can include provisions for employment, or regional or social objectives. Despite this possibility, we came across few signs of such a social dimension being built directly into the 1992 regulatory framework; instead it has been dealt with separately in the Social Charter of the EC and its implementing programme. In Germany, the commitment to social consensus is a powerful force opposing any deregulatory chain reaction in the field of social policy. This is true of other member-states with Christian Democratic traditions or strong socialist or social democratic movements and is simply not understood in Britain. Although the picture in the social field is mixed, there seems little doubt that the British voluntarist approach (whether in the form of self-regulation of markets or negotiated collective bargaining at company level) will come under growing pressure from EC legislation.

Finally, as regards the role of interest groups in influencing the shape of 1992 legislation, it is open to question whether British interest groups, in the post-corporatist climate created in Britain, have either the desire or the ability to make an effective input into the European debate. This, together with the generally negative position on European integration often ascribed to the British by their partners in the EC and the limited clout of British industry, means that their interest groups have an uphill battle when it comes to influencing the shape of the post-1992 regulatory framework. This must be contrasted with the much greater influence of the German economic actors, as a result both of their involvement in domestic-policy formation and of their real weight in the EC economy.

The overall conclusion of the study is that the combination of market-led and policy-led forces has indeed produced a momentum to achieve a single European market. National-market structures are being progressively undermined, but this will not make all local-market characteristics disappear. Local-market presence and traditional exporting strengths will continue to be at a premium. The macro approach to regulation in the EC will be closer to the German *Ordnungspolitik*, which limits day-to-day political intervention, than to the British pattern of giving considerable discretionary power to central government. This is not because Germany exerts some form of dominance within the Community, but for the simple reason that none of the member-states are prepared to see a transfer of discretionary power to the EC. At the micro level, however, the approach will be closer to the British model, and

Review of findings

Germany, which has not moved as far or as fast as Britain towards deregulation during the 1980s, faces more pressure for change in order to bring its policies in line with EC developments.

2
MERGERS AND ACQUISITIONS

One of the means by which the national markets are being integrated into a single European market is through cross-border mergers and acquisitions (M&As). The pressure for M&As has been essentially market-led, with companies coming to the view that reliance on national markets was too constraining if they were to compete internationally. Once the 1992 programme had gained momentum in 1988 and 1989, the number of cross-border M&As increased significantly. This prompted policymakers to resolve the issues that for sixteen years had prevented adoption of a merger-control regulation, namely: what the division of competence between the Community and the member-states should be; and whether policy should be based purely on competition criteria or whether it should also take account of other policy objectives, such as the international competitiveness of European industry.

The increase in cross-border M&As has also raised important questions about the circumstances in which takeovers take place. Within the EC there are two very distinct approaches to takeovers. On the one hand, there is the British approach, which focuses on the rights of shareholders and makes it easy for British-owned companies to be purchased. This has resulted in what has been called an 'open market for corporate control'. On the other hand, many continental companies have a structure of ownership and participation that make takeovers much less common as a means of corporate restructuring. These contrasting approaches raise two policy issues: Should there be an open market for corporate control within the EC? And, if so, can EC legislation bring this about?

Divergences in policy and practice

When the Treaty of Rome was signed in 1957, merger control did not figure high on the agenda of national policymakers. There were provisions covering restrictive agreements and abuse of market power in the form of Articles 85 and 86 (EEC), but no direct merger control.[1] At this time, there was a tendency among national governments to promote rather than control mergers, since they regarded them as a useful means of helping European industry to recover its international competitiveness. Furthermore, no formal merger controls existed in any of the member-states; Britain was the first European country to introduce pre-merger controls in the Monopolies and Mergers Act of 1965.

By the early 1970s, there was a growing concern about the impact of increasing industrial concentration on both competition and competitiveness, and there were moves to introduce pre-merger controls at both national and EC levels. In 1973, the European Commission made its initial proposals for a merger-control regulation at the same time as the German legislation was introduced.[2] The Commission's proposals made little progress, partly because member governments were reluctant to cede the relevant powers to Brussels, and partly because of differing approaches to merger control.

The French, Italians and British were reluctant to accept EC merger regulation because it would have restricted their ability to pursue national industrial, regional or social policy objectives. The Germans and Danes, on the other hand, favoured the use of strict competition criteria when assessing mergers. They were prepared to accept an EC regulation, but only if it precluded the use of merger policy as an instrument of industrial policy.

The approach adopted in the German legislation of 1973 was to separate the regulation of competition policy from the political arena. Responsibility for the day-to-day implementation of competition policy, including pre-merger control of industrial concentrations, was therefore placed with the independent Federal Cartel Office (Bundeskartelamt) in Berlin. This uses fairly tightly defined criteria about markets and their structures to prohibit those mergers that would result in the establishment of market dominance. The Minister of Economics retains reserve powers to overrule the decision of the Cartel Office, but these have been used only seven times since 1973. The recent highly controversial case in which ministerial powers were used to allow the Daimler-MBB merger must be seen against this background.

In contrast, the statutory basis of British policy provides for the flexible and discretionary use of the concept of public interest. Since 1984, however, the British Conservative government has pursued a policy of referring bids to the Monopolies and Mergers Commission (MMC), primarily, if not exclusively, on competition grounds. The law still allows reference to public interest, but successive ministers have exercised self-restraint and have yielded less frequently to pressures to refer bids for political reasons. British policy on mergers thus depends on the views of the government of the day. A change of government could well result in a shift to more intervention in the pursuit of national industrial-policy objectives, provided that this is still possible under EC law.

Other member-states that have some form of national merger control tend to follow an approach based on public interest, and have in the past used mergers as instruments of industrial policy. This was and remains the case in France, although the competition authorities have been shifting towards a more competition-based approach. Italy has no national merger-control provision, although legislation has been pending in the Senate for some time now. The Spanish are in the process of introducing their own national legislation. This is at least in part because of the rapid industrial restructuring that is taking place as a result of EC membership. In the other smaller countries there is more reliance on an open-trade stance as the means to ensure competition, since it often takes only a small degree of concentration to produce monopolistic industrial structures on the national market. It is therefore in their interest to have an effective EC control mechanism.

In 1976, the Commission presented a revised draft of the merger-control proposal to placate member-states that were opposed to any shift in competence to the EC. Its suggestion was to use thresholds so as to sift out cross-border mergers more easily. It also proposed a form of shared decision-making between member-states and the Commission, whereby the Commission would assess proposed mergers, but a majority of member-states could, if they disagreed with the decision, refer the case to the Council of Ministers. The German government opposed this, fearing that it could be used by their more interventionist partners to pursue European industrial policy objectives. An amended draft, produced in 1982, clarified the competence issue further by leaving national authorities to exercise the control when both companies concerned held a high percentage of their assets in the same member-state. But still no progress could be made in the Council. When the 1985 White Paper on the completion of the internal market was drawn up it contained no reference to merger control.

There are also fundamental differences in the general environment within which acquisitions and takeovers occur. Britain, as noted above, has an open market for corporate control. There are a number of reasons for this, one of which is that a particularly large proportion of British companies are listed and traded on the London Stock Exchange and thus are available for purchase. Capitalization of the London Stock Exchange is equivalent to 98% of the national GDP, compared with only 20% in France and Germany, and 16% in Italy. In Italy, because of family shareholdings and various defensive pacts, only a few of the 200 companies listed can be bought.[3] France is generally more open and there are a fair number of takeovers, but the state continues to hold 15% of all shares. Another factor is that the ready availability of information about British companies makes it easier to identify and assess potential takeover targets. Regulation by the Takeover Panel in Britain significantly limits defensive gambits by management. The Panel also aims to avoid discriminating between shareholders.

In Germany there is no open market for corporate control. Compared with France and Italy, Germany has far fewer structural barriers to takeover, but the whole environment is one that tends to foster commitment to the company rather than provide incentives to sell up. All major stakeholders – including the major banks and insurance companies, which hold about 20% of all shares in the large joint-stock companies – and employees, through their participation on the supervisory board, are directly involved in the future of the company. The would-be purchaser also has to clear some formidable hurdles in order to gain effective control of a German company. For example, members of the supervisory board of a German company are appointed for five years, and 75% of voting shares are needed to change the supervisory board. German company law also allows there to be as many non-voting shares as voting shares. Finally, a number of vulnerable companies, such as the Feldmühle – the target of the first hostile bid in the FRG – can limit voting rights for any shareholder to 5% or 10%, regardless of the size of the holding.

Merger-and-acquisition activity

The overall pattern of M&A activity shows that cross-border links, both within Western Europe* and internationally, have accounted for 30-35%

*The term 'Western Europe' is used throughout this study to mean both EC and EFTA countries.

of all mergers.[4] The range is from about 40% for the Federal Republic of Germany to 10% in the Netherlands, while Britain and France each have a share of about one-third. This contrasts with the United States, where cross-border takeovers, inward and outward combined, have averaged about 12%, and Japan, where the share of foreign acquisitions varied between 0% and 8% in the years 1984–6.

In 1988, Britain accounted for no less than 73% of all takeovers in the EC, measured by value, compared with Germany's 4%.[5] In the same year, British companies were also targets in 23 of a total of 26 hostile takeovers recorded in the EC, worth £6,483m out of a total of £7,342m. Most of these were British companies buying other British companies, but all three of the cross-border hostile bids in that year targeted British companies. The same figures show that British acquisitions were greater in number but of a smaller scale, with the result that there was a rough balance in value of about £2.5bn either way. This may demonstrate that it is difficult to acquire major or strategic companies in other member-states, or it may reflect a cautious approach on the part of British companies to taking over 'European' companies.

Interviews during 1989 suggested that British companies saw a growing threat of foreign takeover as more firms in the EC responded to the challenge of the single market. Early figures for 1989 seemed to support this view. For example, one survey showed that British companies accounted for 20.8bn ecus out of the total of 45.3bn ecus or, in numerical terms, 237 of a total of 1,300 reported cross-border acquisitions in Western Europe.[6] The major predators seem to be from companies outside the EC. US companies, which made acquisitions totalling 13.8bn ecus in the EC in 1988, accounted for 75% of the British companies that were taken over. French companies had been very active in the M&A markets during 1988, but they were surpassed by German companies during the second half of 1989. This may be due to a few big German deals, such as Siemens' takeover, together with Britain's General Electricity Company, of Plessey, and Deutsche Bank's acquisition of Morgan Grenfell, but it is an indication that, as expected, German companies are becoming more active in M&As as a result of the competitive challenge of 1992.

The regulation to control mergers
In 1986, the Commission produced a draft proposal in response to the market-led pressure for an EC merger-control regulation.[7] In the fol-

lowing year, the ECJ ruled on a decision taken by the Commission on the basis of Article 85 (EEC), in which the Commission challenged an arrangement between Philip Morris and Rothmans to acquire another company. The Commission argued that the companies had infringed Article 85(1) (EEC). Although it did not uphold all of the Commission's arguments, the ECJ's judgment was interpreted by many, including the Commission, as supporting the view that Article 85 (EEC) could be used to block certain mergers.

These developments showed both that the Commission was determined to have a say in merger control and that it could well receive ECJ backing. For business this meant multiple – i.e. EC and national – control, with the attendant increased costs and uncertainties at precisely the time when more companies were considering cross-border takeovers. For example, the Siemens-GEC bid for Plessey was considered by the Office of Fair Trading (OFT) and the MMC in Britain, by the Federal Cartel Office in Germany, and by the European Commission, not to mention further notifications in Australia, Canada, South Africa and the United States, mainly because of defence interests. Seven different law firms were employed preparing papers.[8] In this case all these agencies came to more or less the same view, but the existence of different national regimes and the risk that they could reach different conclusions were clearly seen as a threat to cross-border restructuring. When the Commission tabled its 1986 proposal, several governments, including the French, maintained a formal reserve. By early 1988, however, the French had shifted position out of recognition of the need for industry to restructure across Europe in order to establish a strong base from which to compete with US and Japanese firms. To compete with other global players, French firms had to become global players themselves, and national controls in other EC countries were seen as an obstacle to this aim. The German position favoured an EC regulation, provided that it was based on competition criteria and not on 'industrial policy' objectives. The British reserved their position.

As in earlier debates there were two key issues: Community competence and the criteria to be applied. On the first point, entrepreneurs, the Commission and all member-states were keen to avoid double or multiple control. Therefore, unless the officials of the Commission's DG IV (the directorate-general responsible for competition policy) were to assume control of all mergers, a measure that no one supported, there had to be a demarcation between national and Community control. This could be achieved only with exclusive Community competence for mergers between companies with combined worldwide turnover that was above a specific threshold. The higher the threshold the fewer the mergers that would be covered by Community competence and therefore the greater the role for the national authorities.

It soon became clear that the German position was crucial. During its presidency of the Council in the first half of 1988, the German government had given its support, in principle, to the proposed regulation. But by mid-1988 it became clear that there were serious misgivings, above all in the Federal Cartel Office, about ceding exclusive powers to the Commission. When it seemed that Peter Sutherland, the Commissioner responsible, had gained agreement on exclusivity from the Ministry of Economics, the Cartel Office entered the public debate and argued strongly against the proposal.[9]

The Cartel Office's case rested on three arguments. First, it claimed that the proposed EC regulation would be weaker than existing German measures. These prohibit, for example, the attainment of market dominance and can operate even in the case of minority holdings of 25% of voting shares. The Community provision bites only when there is a change of control. Second, the EC proposal did not follow the German policy of separating the consideration of competition from political factors. The Germans saw this as a vital means of avoiding situations in which covert pressure could be brought to bear on the Commission. And, third, the criteria proposed for assessing bids could permit the merger control to become an instrument of European industrial policy. The German government therefore sought to limit Community competence significantly by retaining parallel national controls and insisting on a high threshold of 10bn ecus.

Although the British government took no formal position until well into 1989, it was actively involved in negotiations with the Germans and the French on the shape of the proposal. British preoccupations centred on a desire to retain as much flexibility as possible on how to determine national public interest. Only a narrow definition of national public interest, covering security, plurality of media and prudential rules (Article 21 of the final regulation), could be agreed. The British would ideally have liked to retain a general public-interest clause in the EC regulation, but when this proved impossible they switched to trying to prevent the transfer of discretionary powers to the Community. As the negotiations proceeded, they also moved to support exclusive competence for the Community, but above relatively high thresholds so as to avoid double control.

Peter Sutherland, who had played such an important role in promoting the regulation, tabled a revised draft in December 1988 just before leaving the Commission.[10] In March 1989, the new Commissioner, Sir Leon Brittan, raised the thresholds to 5bn ecus on combined worldwide turnover and 66% for the national-merger test. Smaller member-states were less than happy with this, and a compromise proposed by the Commission and supported by the French was for a 5bn ecus threshold for the initial period and a subsequent reduction to 2bn.

This compromise proposal formed the basis for the final agreement. The lower threshold of 100m ecus was, however, increased to 250m. The Commission would control mergers in which the combined Community turnover of at least two of the companies concerned exceeded this limit, which is to be reviewed after four years on the basis of a qualified majority vote.[11] The German government fought to retain double or parallel national control and appeared prepared to consider vetoing the regulation unless it got some satisfaction.[12] In the end, what came to be called the 'German clause' was included in the regulation. Article 9 provides that the Commission may refer a case to a national competition authority if the latter requests this because it wishes to consider the impact of a merger on certain geographical reference markets (i.e. national markets), even when the proposed concentration falls within the thresholds and when the Commission would otherwise allow it to proceed. If the national authority concludes that the merger would be anti-competitive, it must refer the case back to the Commission, which may then either deal with it itself or ask the national authority to investigate further or act. This elaborate procedure provides for a degree of national competence to remain. This provision, too, will be reviewed after four years, but, much to the displeasure of a number of member-states, especially Britain, unanimity will be required to change it (i.e. to remove it).

As a result of these political compromises, residual double control will remain for some 40–50 cases likely to fall under the EC merger controls each year. This will not please European industrialists and is contrary to the objectives of the Commission. In addition, Articles 85 and 86 (EEC) remain in force for all mergers below the thresholds in the merger regulation. The new regulation required the Commission to refrain from initiating recourse to Articles 85 and 86 (EEC), but these articles grant rights to individuals, who may still bring cases. It is unlikely that the ECJ would entertain an action under Articles 85 or 86 (EEC) concerning a merger which fell within the scope of the EC merger regulation. However, with the threshold set so high, a good many mergers risk being in double jeopardy. In many cases, companies will probably feel that it is safer to notify a merger to both the national authorities and the Commission. In other words, industry has not got the one-stop shop it wanted.

The other key issue was the criteria to be applied in judging mergers. Initially, the Commission had proposed including criteria allowing it to approve a merger that would impede effective competition within the EC, provided that it contributed to other objectives of the Treaty, such as 'improving production and distribution, promoting technical or economic progress, or improving the competitive structure within the common market'. In the eyes of the British and German authorities this would have been an invitation to use the regulation to promote European industrial policy objectives. The French and Italians supported the proposal, as did many large European companies, since they wanted the Commission to have the flexibility to take account of factors relevant to international competitiveness. The differences between, on the one hand, the Germans and the British, and, on the other, the French, were thrashed out in informal meetings in early 1989. The Germans and the British prevailed, arguing from experience with their own highly developed merger-control policies. The criteria subsequently adopted in the regulation were therefore significantly tightened up. Article 2 contains no provision empowering the Commission to allow a merger that impedes effective competition. The Commission may take account of the development of technical and economic progress, but only if this is to the consumer's advantage and not an obstacle to competition.

Again in line with their national practice, the Germans argued for the creation of a separate and politically independent competition authority. The Federal Cartel Office believed that this would be the only certain way of ensuring that the Commission was not open to political influence. British views were less clear-cut. The competition agencies broadly followed the German line, with the MMC floating ideas for a Euro–MMC, whereas the British government favoured an open and transparent process, but not a new institution. One option that has been under consideration would be to create an independent unit within the Commission. This may be an option for the future, but much will depend on how the regulation is applied in the first four years.[13]

The opposition to granting discretionary powers to the Commission must be put in context. Past experience with Articles 85 and 86 (EEC) suggests that national authorities are far more likely than the Commission to be subject to 'political influence' in the pursuit of industrial policy objectives. By restricting the powers of the Commission, the liberal member-states merely leave more scope for 'interventionist' national policies. Where the Commission has been subject to political influence, as in the field of state aids, this pressure has generally taken the form of the national governments seeking to prevent the Commission using tough competition criteria, rather than to prevent it pursuing industrial policies. Thus it seems unlikely that narrowly defined criteria contained in the regulation will ever be used to pursue EC industrial policy objectives.

The agreement on a European merger-control regulation, effective from 21 September 1990, is a significant step towards creating a coherent merger policy for the single market. The agreement is closer to the German model than any other, but it is essentially a convergence of the individual member-states' positions. It should be stressed, however, that the emphasis on competition criteria leaves little or no scope for the consideration of social issues, such as the impact of mergers on regional employment. Finally, it is worth noting the third-country provisions in Article 24 of the regulation. These require the Commission to draw up a report by September 1991 on the treatment of concentrations in non-member countries. If this report shows that these countries do not grant Community companies treatment 'comparable to that granted by the Community' to companies in foreign countries, the Commission *may* submit proposals for negotiations with a view to obtaining comparable treatment. In addition, the regulation allows the Commission to seek undertakings that any merger outside the EC would not endanger effective competition. However, these third-country mergers will have to be notified to the Commission when the EC market is affected.

A level playing-field

A central question in the debate is whether companies will be subject to similar regimes across the whole of the EC. There are two main issues: how to ensure that companies in one part of the Community are not subject to tougher or laxer competition tests than elsewhere; and how to ensure that the playing-field for takeovers is level throughout the EC. On the first point, the adoption of the merger-control regulation is only a part of the solution, since below the thresholds it is the national controls that will determine whether a merger can go ahead or not. A genuine level playing-field cannot be achieved without the alignment of national competition policies. At present there is considerable diversity in the national controls. Whereas some countries have none, at the opposite end of the scale the German authorities see thorough controls as contributing to the competitiveness of German companies, since competition is deemed the best means of ensuring competitiveness. The absence of national merger controls in some member-states could create distortions. In Spain, for example, there has been some political concern that rapid restructuring without the safety net of national controls would put Spanish companies at risk.

What are the chances of national policies converging? In the field of restrictive business practices, in which the provisions in Articles 85 and 86 (EEC) have been in force since 1958, there has been significant convergence. Revisions of national legislation almost always build on the EC approach, as did, for example, the 1987 review of British restrictive-trade practices. In Spain and Italy the new national legislation is being designed to complement the EC regulation. But when it comes to long-established national policies there has been less success. During the 1980s, even though the restrictive-trade practices in Britain were very similar to those in Germany, the statutory bases of their policies were very different. In both countries there have recently been revisions of national policy in advance of the outcome of the EC debate, and neither country has paid much, if any, attention to the implications of EC legislation. It therefore looks likely that, in spite of the agreement at the EC level, national differences will persist for some time, and the greater the number of mergers that fall under national control, the greater the scope for conflict.

The second and probably more important issue is the absence of a level playing-field for takeovers in the EC. As already noted, it is mainly British companies that feel vulnerable, because of the open market for corporate control in Britain. A level playing-field can be created in one of two ways: either through the impact of market forces or through EC rules to harmonize procedures for takeovers and company law. There is not much evidence of market-led factors, either global or European, producing a rapid or significant convergence of the diverse national environments for takeovers. Some argue that pressures to liberalize financial markets elsewhere in the EC so as to reduce the costs of equity finance will eventually bring about more open markets for companies elsewhere, but this seems doubtful.[14] First, and this was borne out by interviews carried out in Germany, industrialists are not likely to see any merit in adopting the British model, which has so obviously failed to ensure consistent growth and industrial competitiveness. Second, the US experience with the British open market for takeovers has been unsuccessful, and there are pressures to erect barriers to takeover, especially at state level, rather than to remove them. Therefore the general international climate is not favourable towards liberalization.[15]

Prospects of convergence led by deliberate policy change look equally doubtful, although some progress was made in July 1988 with the agreement on a Community provision covering disclosure of major shareholdings. This requires that there is notification of those share transfers that result in holdings of greater than 10%. This will be followed by further notifications at 20%, 33%, 50% and 60%. The Federal Republic (which currently has a 25% threshold) voted against this in the EC Council, but was overridden in a qualified majority vote. In December 1988 the Commission, urged on by the British, drafted the Thirteenth Company Law Directive, which seeks to harmonize takeover procedures in the EC.[16] This proposed that any shareholder seeking a stake beyond a 33% threshold must make a formal bid for the company, and that companies must provide appropriate offer-documents and limits on certain 'poison-pill' defences. But Britain pressed for more and got the Commission to agree to conduct a fuller study of barriers to takeovers.[17] In its report, the Commission recognized that takeovers had a positive role in industrial restructuring. It recommended amendments to the Thirteenth and Fifth Company Law Directives in order further to limit defensive tactics, such as purchasing a company's own shares during a public takeover battle or restricting the voting rights of shareholders.[18] But these proposals will not bite on the underlying structural barriers.

The British government has made all the running on the case for common provisions on takeovers. The logic of EC legislation, however, is that the City of London's Takeover Panel would lose its voluntary status, a prospect that has caused some concern in the City. It would indeed be a paradox if the British opposed the Thirteenth Company Law Directive, which is modeled on the City's Takeover Code, in order to defend the voluntarist, self-regulation of the City. Another source of doubt in British minds is that many barriers to takeover, especially in Germany, depend on company law which the British are reluctant to see harmonized. British business and the Conservative government are also dedicated to defending 'voluntarism' in labour relations. They have developed a Pavlovian reaction to proposals for EC company law; an *Angst* at the German worker-participation approach wells up as soon as the topic is mentioned.[19] The Commission's proposals on, for example, the voting rights of shareholders, which are important for a level playing-field for takeovers, are in the draft Fifth Company Law Directive, the very directive that touches the rawest British nerves on worker participation. These factors necessarily dampen British enthusiasm for European harmonization of relevant national legislation. Since the rest of the Community has no great interest in changing the status quo, one must doubt that policy-led changes will be very substantial.

Continued divergence between the British and the German (or continental) models is highly relevant to whether national industrial sovereignty will persist in the EC in the sense of nationals retaining ownership of key industries or companies. By its rules to defend the open market for the control of companies, British regulatory policy is implicitly ceding national industrial sovereignty. The Germans have no policy designed explicitly to prevent foreign ownership, but the German model does ensure that all stakeholders, who are in most cases German, retain a long-term commitment to the company. In this way national industrial sovereignty is effectively retained. The position in the other member-states is closer to the German than the British model. British companies and regulators will therefore have to accept the logic of the 'competition-among-rules' approach embodied in the 1992 programme. If the continental approach prevails, the British will either have to change policy or continue to face an unlevel playing-field and the loss of industrial sovereignty.

Conclusions
It was the market-led increase in cross-border mergers and takeovers which resulted in the merger-control regulation being finally adopted after sixteen years. Cross-border M&As were already bringing closer a real single market. The ECJ has worked with the grain of market pressures in its decisions, and thus played a key role by persuading the member-states to agree the new regulation. Whether this combination of market factors and EC legislation will result in an increase in competition is still too early to say, since in some sectors Europe-wide oligopolies will replace national oligopolies. A single market for corporate control is not, however, likely to be achieved, and structural barriers will remain for the foreseeable future.

The merger-control regulation represents a degree of reregulation at the EC level. It was recognized that national regulation was no longer appropriate and that it had to be supplemented or replaced at the EC level. The radical deregulation approach would have been to remove national controls altogether, but the member-states were not prepared to go so far. Nor were they willing to transfer any discretionary powers to the EC, with the result that the merger-control regulation does not provide a basis for an EC-wide industrial policy. The regulation constitutes a kind of deregulation in that it removed the discretionary powers of national governments to use merger control as an instrument of industrial policy for large mergers and did not replace this with EC-level discretionary power. On takeovers there has been a modest degree of reregulation, pushed by the British, in order to try to establish a common set of rules for takeovers in the EC.

It is in line with both British and German policy objectives that the single market and its merger policy be competition based. By agreeing to the merger-control regulation, the British have accepted permanent limitations on their ability to use discretionary powers based on public interest. Although the regulation caused the Federal Cartel Office to make painful concessions on detail and the Commission is still seen as not independent enough, the fundamental structure of the merger-control regulation is fully consistent with the German approach.

3

PUBLIC PROCUREMENT

This chapter considers the efforts in the EC to liberalize public procurement. In so doing it focuses on two aspects of the EC's work: measures to achieve compliance with market-liberalizing measures; and the extension of the Community regime to cover the strategically important utilities sectors of energy, transport, telecommunications and water. The liberalization of procurement markets constitutes a major part of the 1992 programme. Total public procurement in the EC accounts for about 15% of Community GDP. Only part of this, to a value of between 250bn ecus and 360bn ecus (1987), or 7%-10% of EC GDP, is subject to individual contracts and thus potentially open to competition. The 'cost of non-Europe' study estimated that open markets for these would yield a total potential saving of between 8 and 19bn ecus per annum.[1] The opening of these markets, in particular for the excluded utilities sectors, which account for about one-third of procurement and are dominated by national champions, constitutes a major challenge. If successful, this would have a considerable impact on competition and on the structure of European industry.

The nature and scale of the task
The Community has been seeking to open procurement markets for some time. Article 30 (EEC) prohibits quantitative restrictions or measures with equivalent effect. Since explicit 'buy-national' policies can be seen as having an effect equivalent to a quantitative restriction, they have always been deemed contrary to Article 30 (EEC). In the 1970s, direc-

tives were adopted in an effort to implement the treaty provisions in the field of public-works (i.e. construction) and public-supplies (investment goods and equipment) contracts. These had little effect during the economic recession of the 1970s when defensive national measures were prevalent, such as the use of national design standards, interpretive 'tricks' to keep tenders outside the scope of the directives, the widespread use of exceptions to exclude foreign and non-traditional suppliers, and the fragmenting of contracts in order to keep below the EC thresholds. Furthermore, there were no effective provisions to ensure compliance, and key strategic sectors, such as power plants, telecommunications and transport, were excluded. In addition to these weaknesses in legislation, and equally important, was the fact that market-opening lacked credibility. Suppliers were disinclined to waste time and money bidding for foreign contracts that they were convinced they would not get.

Markets therefore remained closed. In 1985, for example, foreign suppliers accounted for only 4% of German, 0.3% of Italian and 0.4% of British total public orders, which amounted to about 20% for these economies as a whole.[2] A French study of public-works contracts shows that in 1986 contractors from other EC countries had gained 3.2% of the French market, 2.9% of the German, 1.8% of the British, 1.5% of the Spanish and a negligible share of the Italian contracts.[3]

Oligopolistic behaviour acts as a brake on market-opening. In the excluded sectors the costs for research and development (R&D) are typically high, and patterns of demand are cyclical or irregular. As a result, suppliers are wary about market-opening that threatens the *oligopolistic structure of markets*. Even when they accept change, they prefer an orderly transition from national oligopolies to oligopolistic market structures, whether on a European or on an international scale. None of the British and German suppliers interviewed in 1989 believed that the EC directives would have an immediate liberalizing effect. But British suppliers, who were being forced to adjust to privatization and liberal procurement policies at home, were more prepared to accept radical change than German suppliers, who had both a larger national market and comfortable access to public contracts.

Structure of purchasing also differs between countries and sectors. Generally speaking, purchasing is rather centralized in France and Britain, and decentralized in Germany and Italy. Electricité de France (EDF), for example, accounts for virtually all power-equipment purchases in France. In Britain, privatization is leading to some decentralization of purchasing, but still to a lesser extent than in Germany, where energy and water procurement, for example, is spread over a large number of utilities, many very small. Power generators in Germany range from the very large Rheinland Westfälisches Elektrizitätswerke (RWE), with nuclear power stations, to the Black Forest sawmills, which sell surplus hydroelectric power to the local utility. The railways and telecommunications sectors are unusual in being subject to centralized purchasing in most member-states.

Differing structures of ownership are a special problem in the case of the utilities, which explains why these were excluded from the directives of the 1970s. The French and Italians have relied almost exclusively on nationalized industries. In Britain, the only utility that is not yet privately owned is British Rail. In Germany there is a mixture of public, private and joint ownership of energy and water, although rail transport and telecommunications remain publicly owned. Interestingly there is no clear correlation between private ownership and open markets. It is, however, generally assumed that privatization brings open markets. This seems to be confirmed in Britain, where 25% of recent orders by British Telecom for public switching equipment have gone to foreign suppliers, and the power-generating companies have bought Siemens gas-powered generating sets.

Size of operation does not seem to be a determining factor. Interviews suggested that local utility companies, part-owned by local government and with local politicians on their supervisory boards, are no more immune to the political pressures to 'buy local' than any fully nationalized utility. It is for these reasons that the Commission argued that European rules must embrace private as well as public companies.

The *legal structures* governing public purchasing and remedies against illegal practices vary considerably across the EC. Some countries, such as France and Italy, have detailed administrative law and administrative courts. Others, such as Britain and Denmark, have no administrative courts, and redress must be sought either informally via a member of parliament or local councillor or by application to a high court for judicial review. Germany is a special case because its Basic Law is interpreted as requiring public purchasing to be governed by private law and thus precludes any intervention by a public body to enforce compliance. In theory all member-states provide some form of remedy, but these are seldom, if ever, used. Many countries provide for damages, and in Spain, Greece and Denmark, for example, powers exist to suspend contract-award procedures while irregularities are corrected. But national remedies are inadequate and costly, and suppliers are naturally reluctant to take a potential customer to court. The EC directives on supplies and works in the 1970s helped little because they were not accompanied by efforts to align national remedies, depending instead on national administrative guidelines, which provided no legal rights for individual companies.

In their *purchasing practices*, purchasers have shown a clear preference to buy from companies that have a local-market presence. This is often justified on the grounds that this facilitates rapid repairs and thus reduces reserve capacity and costs. Purchasers also prefer dealing in one language with a few suppliers, since this fosters close co-operation in R&D. Purchasers typically retain two to four approved suppliers, enabling them to retain close supplier-purchaser links while maintaining competition. One example gleaned in interviews in the German power industry illustrates the point: rationalization of production in a certain range of power transformers resulted in a reduction in the number of suppliers for a major utility from three to two. The purchaser wanted to find a new supplier to ensure continued competition, but, rather than find a supplier elsewhere in the EC, the utility encouraged another local supplier to invest in capacity to produce the product concerned. Similar practices are used throughout the EC. Indeed, purchasers will argue that they see no reason why EC legislation should force them to change practices that are efficient, only to incur additional costs in the process.

Decades of close supplier-purchaser links have resulted in distinctive national *design standards*. In utilities, the whole national network is often based on a specific technology, which limits the scope for economies of scale and fragments the European market. The existence of these national design standards has meant that neither purchasers nor suppliers have had a strong interest in devising European, or for that matter international, standards. As a result, standard-making in the excluded sectors lags far behind current market trends towards the internationalization of supply. It has been estimated that some 5,000 standards are needed to cover the excluded sectors, yet only about 1,000 exist. Where technological change is relatively fast, as in telecommunications, the situation is more dynamic; the life cycle of the technology is between five and fifteen years for terminal or switching equipment. But in other sectors, such as railways or power distribution, the life-cycle of equipment can be as much as twenty or twenty-five years. Producers that have developed the technologies together with the network operators will clearly have better market access.

Finally, there are the *political issues*. All member-states use public procurement to promote social, regional and industrial policy objectives. The subjective judgment inevitably involved in any purchasing decision has enabled governments to pursue implicit industrial policies. Contract compliance provisions are often used to tackle unemployment or other social objectives. There have been regional preferences in procurement in Northern Ireland and in the inner-German border zone and Berlin, which, like other regional preferences in the EC, are likely to be permitted until 1992. Italy had a law requiring 40% of all public procurement to be placed with companies in the Mezziogiorno. A recent ECJ decision in the *Dupont de Nemours* case has ruled that the Italian law is contrary to the Treaty of Rome. This throws into question the legality of all such national policies.

Market-led change
During the late 1970s and early 1980s, industrial restructuring on a national scale was clearly reaching its limits, yet national ways of thinking were so deeply entrenched that cross-border rationalization was not seen as a credible alternative. But the rising costs of R&D began to change this view. In the early 1980s, West European telecommunications companies spent $7bn developing eight different kinds of public switching system. US companies spent $3bn developing two, and the Japanese $2bn developing one. Everyone knew that the next generation of technology would be even more expensive, so the companies accepted that industrial restructuring would have to spill over national frontiers. Even then they were reluctant, and it took an outsider, American Telephone and Telegraph (AT&T), to precipitate change when it sought to establish itself on the European market by means of a joint venture with Philips and, later, Olivetti. Companie Général d'Electricité (CGE) responded by buying ITT's operations in Europe, including Standard Elektrik Lorenz (SEL), one of the German 'court' suppliers to the Bundespost, to create Alcatel. Siemens, prevented by German cartel laws from buying the ITT operations, responded in 1989 by acquiring Plessey by means of a joint venture with GEC. It was judged necessary to have presence across Western Europe in order to compete and the quickest way of doing this was to acquire local companies.

There was a similar picture in the heavy-electrical-equipment industry, which supplied power utilities. For example, in 1987 Western Europe had ten manufacturers of turbine generators, compared with only two in the United States. This time it was the Swedish company ASEA that precipitated cross-border restructuring when it acquired, first, the Swiss-German Brown-Boveri and then, in 1988, Ansaldo of Italy; the resultant company, ASEA Brown-Boveri (ABB), had annual sales in heavy electrical equipment of $18 billion in 1988, well ahead of Siemens with $11 billion. In response, Alsthom of France and GEC of Britain merged their power divisions in 1988.[4] Such restructuring must be seen as part of an effort to increase global competitiveness by strengthening the 'domestic' base in Europe. ABB has, for example, also made purchases in the United States in order to gain access to that market.

Even the highly diversified construction industry is undergoing a process of acquisition-led restructuring. In this sector, which accounts for one-third of all public procurement within the EC, it is particularly important to distinguish the impact of market-led developments on different-sized companies. Competition is global in the field of major project-management contracts. Much of the actual construction work is then sub-contracted to local firms. In so diverse a sector, it is often difficult to identify which company has led the change, but French companies, possibly trying to catch up after being so nationally oriented, appear to have been the most active in recent acquisitions. In an effort to become more global, companies such as Bouygues are actively acquiring market presence across Western Europe.[5] German companies are also active and benefit from a fairly high degree of vertical integration in building products and allied financial services. The British market has been seen as particularly attractive, especially in such areas as the infra-structure for water utilities, in which there is a significant backlog of capital investment and the industry has recently been privatized. The high profit margins in the British construction industry, at least on paper, are a further incentive, although some British question whether British profitability is really what it appears to be.

Although there have been considerable achievements in cross-border restructuring in these exclusive sectors, there are still formidable barriers to market-opening, most of which are non-statutory or structural, and cannot be removed by the wave of the legislators' pen. EC directives can establish common procedures, as well as better and more comparable access to remedies. These measures are unlikely to be enough, even with market-led pressures and the backing of the ECJ, unless there are also changes in the attitudes of both purchasers and suppliers that would reduce some of the non-statutory and structural barriers. The challenge of 1992 in public procurement is therefore how to make market-opening so credible that suppliers will judge it worthwhile to bid for contracts in other member-states and purchasers will become willing to buy abroad. This requires a package of measures covering all sectors and incorporating effective remedies.

Policy-led change: the EC's programme
Public procurement was given a high priority in the Commission's 1985 White Paper. The objectives were: to strengthen the existing directives on supplies and works; to improve the application of rules on compliance; to extend coverage to the so-called excluded sectors; and to liberalize the procurement of services, such as data processing or civil-engineering consultancy. The Commission's action programme in 1986 therefore envisaged five pieces of legislation: a revised works directive and a revised supplies directive; a compliance directive; an excluded sectors (utilities) directive; and a directive on the procurement of services.[6]

The revised supplies and works directives
The Community's approach was influenced by experience with the supplies and works directives during the 1970s, hence the revisions to tighten them up. The directives are important not only in their own right, but also because they served as precedents for the subsequent utilities directive. In order to limit compliance costs with rising inflation, the threshold for works contracts was increased from 1m to 5m ecus. The supplies threshold is bound by the GATT Government Purchasing Agreement. Coverage was extended to prevent evasion by leasing or hire-purchase of equipment. Contract-award procedures were tightened to limit the abuse of single-tender purchasing, but the directives retain for purchasers the choice between negotiated (with chosen suppliers), restricted (with an approved list of suppliers) and open tendering. There have been improvements in the diffusion of information about tenders through enhanced transparency provisions, and references to standards are more precise. If possible, European standards – or national standards implementing them – should be used in contract specifications. On regional- and social-policy issues, the works and supplies directives permit the continuation of national regional preferences in purchasing until 1992.[7] The Commission has since made clear that it then intends to phase out national regional preferences and will probably propose EC regional policy measures to replace them. The European Parliament tried, largely unsuccessfully, to introduce further social provisions.

Comprehensive coverage of utilities

Extending coverage of the EC rules to the structurally diverse utilities was one of the most ambitious and controversial parts of the 1992 programme. Despite the protests of privately owned utilities, ownership could not be the primary criterion for what was to be covered. To exclude private utilities would have left out most British utilities, perhaps half the German (assuming that jointly owned energy utilities were also excluded), but would have included virtually all the French and Italian utilities. This was politically a non-starter. The criterion proposed by the Commission, and ultimately agreed, was independent of ownership and based on the granting of special or exclusive rights to a utility by national or local government. Such rights were judged to provide leverage that could be used to influence procurement decisions and to avoid competition. To prevent wrangling over the interpretation, coverage will in practice be determined by lists of the purchasing entities covered in annexes to the directive.[8]

Coverage is also determined by *thresholds*. The Commission came under pressure from industry, especially purchasers, to set high thresholds for the excluded sectors in order to reduce the number of contracts covered and thus the costs of compliance. The Commission's objective was to cover 20% of the contracts by number, but 80% by value. However, to determine the level at which this could be achieved, the Commission needed data that some utilities refused to provide. The Commission therefore fell back on the precedents set for the supplies and works directives, but set the levels slightly higher for supplies, at 400,000 ecus, against 130,000 ecus.* Weapons, as opposed to general supplies for the forces, are excluded, as is procurement for international organizations, such as the European Telecommunications Satellite Organization (EUTELSAT). Most member-states, including Britain, were prepared to accept this broad coverage. The French wanted to go further than the Commission by including the purchase of electricity, so that it might increase exports to its neighbours, particularly Germany. This was political dynamite because of the massive support given to German coal production by the Hundred-Year Agreement (Jahrehundertvertrag), which guarantees the purchase of German coal by the electricity supply industry. If German utilities had access to lower-cost power from France, most German mines would close. This problem has been accentuated by German unification, which has brought inefficient lignite mining under

---

*The Council common position of February 1990 set a special high threshold of 600,000 ecus for telecommunications supplies.

Federal responsibility. The Commission therefore deferred the issue for the debate on a single market in energy.

The German government sought to limit coverage in a number of important areas. It argued that substitution competition existed as regards different sources of energy (electricity, gas and coal) and transport (road, rail and inland waterways), and therefore that all these sectors should be excluded. Neither the Commission nor the other member governments – above all the French, who chaired the Council during the crucial period at the end of 1989 – were prepared to accept continued exemptions. Broad coverage was needed for agreement. This did not prevent the Germans persisting with the argument, especially for electricity and heat (district heating systems fuelled by power plants), as far as, but not into, the session of the Internal Market Council in February 1990, which adopted the common position. But some of the German concerns about coverage of district heating and smaller generators were recognized in the common position, which excludes heat, power or water when they are produced for a company's own use, provided that no more than 30% is sold to a utility.

The main exclusion sought by the British was for upstream oil and gas. This was also ostensibly on the grounds that competition existed. In reality the 50% expenditure on offshore exploration and production (3.9bn ecus of a total of 8.2bn ecus in 1988) was probably the key consideration. The activities of the Offshore Supplies Office (OSO) has long been seen by the Commission as a classic example of how rights, granted to explore parts of the North Sea, can be used as leverage to influence the purchasing decisions of licensees. A compromise was ultimately reached, in Article 3 of the common position, which allowed for upstream oil and gas to be excluded in return for undertakings that licensing approval would no longer be used to influence procurement and that decisions were non-discriminatory. (At the time of writing, the British government is still to decide whether it will use the option of excluding upstream oil and gas on these conditions when it comes to implementing the directive in UK legislation.) Despite formidable difficulties, the EC in the end adopted a directive with very broad coverage, which offered something for everyone.

As with the supplies and works directives, it soon became apparent that there were not enough European *standards*. It was therefore necessary to allow for derogations until the standard-making processes could catch up. In many utilities the mutual-recognition approach to standard-making (see Chapter 4) does not help because of the need for network interconnectability. But only in telecommunications, in which the EC has pursued more active policies for some time, was a specific standards institute – the European Telecommunications Standards Institute (ETSI) – created (see Chapter 5). In the other sectors, initiatives were taken within CEN and CENELEC.* The standards issues created a major rift between British suppliers, who wanted European standards, and the purchasers, who wished to retain sovereignty in standards and technical specifications. The purchasers prevailed and the British government placed a formal reserve on the obligatory use of European standards. Neither utilities nor suppliers in Germany understood how the use of common standards could cause any problems, and the French government was also concerned that a further exemption on standards could open the door to evasion. The British reserve therefore had little impact, but the continued absence of agreed standards, whether European, international or, for that matter, national, in many of the excluded sectors means that the speed with which markets actually open will depend on progress in this field.

On *purchasing procedures* the Commission accepted the need for flexibility in order to accommodate current purchasing practices using open, restricted and negotiated procedures. Here it faced a commonality of interests between the purchasers and suppliers. For the purchasers, and especially for the Germans, the main objective was the ability to preserve their existing practice of negotiating contracts with a few suppliers. The major 'court' suppliers (i.e., suppliers attendant on the monarchy of the natural monopolies) were also quite happy with the existing practice. In order to ensure that these diverse procedures did not result in evasion, the Commission's proposals sought to ensure transparency by detailed obligations on purchasers to supply information. These were attacked by purchasers as an unacceptable bureaucratic burden. Suppliers saw the benefits in having greater transparency, but also shared some of the fears of purchasers concerning bureaucracy.

The criteria for award of contracts used the broad concept of the 'most economically advantageous' bid. This can be taken to mean more or less anything and can include delivery dates, price, security of supply and after-sales service. The directive is therefore permissive in terms of existing practices and no more likely, by itself, to result in open procurement than the revised works and supplies directives. Much therefore depends on compliance.

*European Standards Committee and European Electrical Standards Committee. Both are known by their French acronyms.

34

Despite the efforts of the European trade unions, backed by the European Parliament, there is little in the directive concerning the *social dimension* of public procurement. The European Trades Union Congress succeeded in getting the European Parliament to make a number of proposals aimed at extending to the European level the kind of policy objectives pursued nationally to promote employment and working conditions through public procurement.[9] On regional preferences, the supplies and works directives again provided the precedent, so that these may remain until 1992. In the context of German unification, this means some form of preference may remain for the new Länder until 1992. This, combined with the fact that the utilities directive will not be implemented until 1993, means that there are two years in which German suppliers can 'sew up' the new and very large market in investment in the utilities of the new Länder. On the other hand, the not insignificant public-works contracts in road-building, etc., carried out by the Federal and Länder governments will be covered by the supplies and works directives.

The compliance directive
The lack of effective compliance was seen as a major reason for the failure of the 1970s directives. The Commission therefore included a compliance directive in its programme.[10] Rather than establish a central regulatory regime, it sought to provide equivalent national remedies and to provide an incentive for aggrieved suppliers to initiate cases, thereby helping to open markets by their own actions. It had a practical side because the Commission was simply not able to monitor the thousands of contracts placed every day. Recognizing that suppliers may not wish to jeopardize their own positions, the Commission also sought powers for itself to intervene, in exceptional circumstances, to suspend contract-award procedures and to ensure that the EC provisions were applied in a similar fashion in all member-states. The core of the directive, however, was to require all member-states to offer the following remedies: speedy interim or interlocutory measures to correct alleged infringements, including suspension of contract-award procedures; the removal of discriminatory technical, economic or financial specifications; and damages for suppliers in cases of infringement.

The directive passed through the European and national parliaments without much debate.[11] By the time it returned to the Council, business lobbies, representing suppliers and especially purchasers in both Britain and Germany, as well as other member-states, had alerted national governments to the disruptive effect on business of contract suspension. The member-states opposed the increase in the Commission's powers associated with EC-level suspension, because this might set a precedent for the Commission to have powers to intervene in national review procedures. The governments prevailed and the discretionary power to suspend contract-award procedures was not awarded to the EC. The member-states retained for themselves the discretion not to suspend or take other interim measures 'where their negative consequences could exceed their benefits'. The Commission managed to keep a so-called corrective mechanism, which enables it to notify member-states in cases of clear and manifest infringement. If member-states fail to correct such infringements, the only remedy would be the somewhat cumbersome Article 169 (EEC) before the ECJ.

Under the directive, adopted by the Council on 22 December 1989, compliance will depend largely on aggrieved suppliers being prepared to bring cases against their potential customers. These will be heard in national administrative or judicial bodies. With one or two notable exceptions, the companies interviewed for this study felt that it was unrealistic to expect them to bite the hand that feeds them in this way. It is therefore by no means certain that the directive will be effective. But a few test cases brought by 'maverick' companies may make the sanctions credible.

Compliance in the excluded sectors
The compliance or remedies directive adopted in December 1989 covers only government procurement proper and not the excluded sectors/ utilities. From the early stages of debate on the excluded sectors it was clear that a separate directive would be needed which took account of the fact that some private-sector companies were to be covered. The Commission's inclination was to stay as close as possible to the remedies directive for supplies and works, but private and mixed-ownership utilities argued that a less interventionist directive had to be developed. German companies and the government argued that, since their purchasing was subject to private law, neither the Commission nor the Federal government could intervene.

The Commission therefore incorporated two additional elements in its proposals.[12] The first drew on the use of audit or attestation proposed by the CBI. The main thrust of these proposals were that:

(a)   the detailed regulations set out in the excluded-sectors directive represented a burden on purchasers, and were in any case inappropriate for private companies;

(b)   the diversity of the sectors covered meant that the use of one directive risked creating a regulatory structure that was inconsistent with market practice; and

(c)   an audit or attestation system would give suppliers more confidence than a set of rules with which purchasers could technically comply, but still pursue parochial purchasing policies.

The second drew on an idea promoted by German industry. This was the establishment of an EC-level conciliation procedure, in which an *ad hoc* body, including industrial representatives, would hear complaints from aggrieved tenderers. Neither attestation nor audit was seen as replacing remedies in the form of damages, or prejudicing rights of action under the directive.

The Commission's proposals thus followed the precedent set by the compliance directive for supplies and works, with rights for individuals to seek remedies from national administrative or judicial bodies, including suspension of contracts, the setting aside of unlawful decisions or claiming damages. As for supplies and works, there was also to be a corrective mechanism, whereby the Commission would bring to the attention of the member-state concerned cases of clear and manifest infringement and seek corrective measures. But attestation may provide an alternative to the suspension of contract-award procedures and is seen as a solution to the German problem of private-contract law. The German idea of a conciliation procedure will enable an individual company to initiate conciliation in a sub-committee of the Advisory Committee for Public Contracts, which would make recommendations. Neither attestation nor conciliation would prejudice the rights of individuals to seek remedies, such as damages.

In incorporating ideas tabled by industry in Germany and in Britain, the Commission has shown itself prepared to work with the private sector. Indeed, the Commission openly discussed drafting with an EC-level Industry Advisory Committee on all the procurement directives. But the procurement case also shows the limits to corporatism at the EC level. Indeed, the various national industrial lobbies were advocating different ideas. The Commission showed considerable skill in playing one off against the other, while using those ideas it found helpful. This strengthened the Commission's hand by enabling it to claim the middle ground. As for the relationship between the Commission and the member-states, the latter combined to prevent the Commission taking on increased discretionary powers, for example the power to suspend contracts. Having lost on this in the compliance directive for supplies and works, the Commission did not try to reintroduce the idea for utilities, but left contract suspension with the member-states.

The excluded-sectors directive succeeded in extending EC rules to almost all sectors and the private utilities. Much more work will, however, have to be done on standards if the sectors concerned are really to open up. When it comes to purchasing practices, the directive is permissive. Purchasers may, if they wish, continue to limit their purchasing to a few local suppliers, assuming local suppliers still exist and have not become part of a European consortium. The directives do not remove the ability of member-states to use procurement for social or regional policy, provided that this does not infringe the treaties, but the Commission intends to suppress such national policies. It remains to be seen whether EC-level social or regional policies emerge. As with supplies and works, much will depend on the compliance provisions in which the Commission is again seeking to extend its powers. It is to be expected that these will be whittled down by opposition from those member-states that resist increased Commission powers, and from industrialists hostile to any form of 'intervention'.

Third-country provisions
The sting in the tail of the excluded-sectors directive lies in the provisions dealing with external aspects. The coverage of the excluded sectors goes far beyond what has been agreed at a multilateral level in GATT. Nor does GATT have anything equivalent to the compliance directives, which offer individual rights for aggrieved suppliers, regardless of nationality. Negotiations parallel to the Uruguay Round of GATT negotiations are under way on broadening the coverage of GATT rules, with the United States especially keen to include telecommunications and power equipment. If the diversity of structure and laws in public procurement is great within the EC, it is even greater within GATT. For example, it is doubtful whether the United States will be prepared to accept multilateral disciplines similar to those included in the EC's excluded-sectors directive, or even coverage of state and local procurement, which accounts for 70% of US public-purchasing.

Because the EC provisions go beyond the current GATT disciplines, the utilities draft directive included a third-country provision. According to this, EC purchasers *may* exclude bidders from the contract-award procedures if the EC content of the products concerned is less than 50%.* In other words companies supplying such products would not have recourse to remedies provided for in the directive. There is also a mandatory 3% price preference for products of EC origin. The Commission justified this with reference to the existence in the United States of federal and state 'buy-American' legislation, which contains price preferences varying between 6% and 25%, and origin tests of 50% in some products. There are similar measures in other OECD countries.

Within the Community, the German government was the main opponent of these third-country provisions. The German concern was twofold: first, products supplied by a number of German companies in the telecommunications sector might not meet the 50% test and therefore not benefit from the directive in selling to the rest of the EC; and, second, a Community measure might result in retaliation by other countries. Both the French and the Italians, with the support of the European Parliament, wanted stronger third-country provisions. The British government opposed the provisions, but accepted that the price of this 'negotiating chip' for the GATT was worth it for an agreement on real steps to liberalize the utilities markets within Europe. At its meeting on 22 December 1989, the Internal Market Council failed to reach agreement, mainly because of this third-country provision. By February 1990, however, the Council established in its common position a procedure whereby the Commission will, during a period beginning in the second half of 1991, produce reports for the Council on developments in the GATT and on practice by the EC's trading partners in the field of government procurement. The Council will then be able to amend the third-country provision by qualified majority. In other words, the Community is linking its third-country provisions to the progress in the GATT negotiations on the Government Purchasing Agreement, and will reconsider the third-country provisions before its own directive is implemented in January 1993.

Conclusion

Global competition is bringing about changes in the structure of European industry in the sectors supplying the utilities covered by the EC's excluded-sectors provisions. Consolidation of the largest firms is taking

*The European Parliament showed a tendency to be more protectionist than the Council by seeking to increase the local-content requirement to 70%.

place across borders and thus putting an end to national champions. The EC's programme of legislation does not have a direct impact on these developments, but it does contribute to confidence that a single market will indeed be achieved. Such confidence is essential for the changes needed in the attitudes of suppliers and purchasers to achieve an effective opening of markets. For smaller companies the directives will, however, be of great importance and will offer a means of breaking into the newly emerging structure of EC-wide markets, which risk replacing national oligopolies by European oligopolies. Much will therefore depend on the willingness of these small operators to use the remedies provided by the directives to force open markets, since the larger operators, with so much to lose, are less likely to do so.

4

TECHNICAL STANDARDS

In the view of many industrialists, the removal of national technical standards should be a top priority on the Community's agenda for the completion of the internal market because of their potential for hindering cross-border trade. The first EC effort to tackle technical harmonization was in 1968, when the Commission's approach to breaking down national standards was to replace them directly with standards that were regulated by the EC. This led to the adoption, between 1969 and 1985, of a total of 270 directives – each full of technical detail.

Since the regulatory capabilities of member-states increased much more quickly than those of the Community, and since negotiations over directives were very time-consuming because of the amount of technical details involved, 'old-approach' directives were often already out of date by the time they were adopted. In addition, many governments were reluctant to accept unconditionally much of the reregulation, fearing that the considerable diversity in existing standards would almost certainly result in compromise, and hence a lowering of standards. Moreover, during the 1970s, political blockages on reasons of 'principle' became more and more frequent, so that the whole process of technical harmonization at Community level came almost to a standstill. In the early 1980s, the Commissions's new approach to technical harmonization and standardization was intended to have a deregulatory bias. In line with the principle of subsidiarity, this approach delegates the maximum possible competence to the voluntary standard-making sector, limiting legislative harmonization to health and safety considerations.

There are complex interactions among three sectors: public agencies, responsible for the legislative aspect of technical harmonization; standard-making bodies, with a private status, which have to fill in the essential safety requirements laid out in the directives; and companies whose products have to meet the essential requirements. This division of labour raises important issues as regards architecture of both the member-states and the EC. Two examples illustrate this. Standards at the European level are made within CEN/CENELEC.* These are private-sector organizations, although they have adopted the same qualified majority voting procedure as the EC Council of Ministers, adapting it to cater for the participation of EFTA countries. CEN/CENELEC standards are not in themselves legally binding, but, if a product is manufactured to a European standard, the enforcement authorities presume its conformity with the essential legal requirements. Another requirement under the information directive (83/189) is that member-states, i.e. public authorities, enforce a standstill on any national – private – standard-making activity which is the subject of a Commission mandate to CEN/CENELEC.[1] European standards also play an increasingly important role in two other areas covered in this volume: public procurement (in which they form one of the major non-statutory barriers to trade) and telecommunications.

This chapter focuses on four directives, the first to implement the new approach:

(1) The simple Pressure Vessels Directive (87/404 EEC), adopted on 25 June 1987, entered into force on 1 July 1990. This was agreed by unanimity and preceded the entry into force of the Single European Act; it has played a pioneering role in establishing the new approach.

(2) The Toy Safety Directive (88/378 EEC), adopted on 3 May 1988, entered into force on 1 January 1990. This is the first application of the new approach to consumer (and, moreover, highly sensitive) products.

(3) The Construction Products Directive (89/106 EEC), adopted on 21 December 1988, scheduled to enter into force by mid-1991. This is particularly interesting because the directive largely covers areas for which in Germany the Länder have exclusive competence.

(4) The Machinery Safety Directive (89/392 EEC), adopted in June 1989, scheduled to enter into force by 31 December 1992. This

*European Standards Committee and European Electrical Standards Committee, both known by their French acronyms.

directive touches the responsibilities of different ministries at the national level, as well as different directorates-general within the Commission. It has also raised issues as to the appropriate legal basis, in particular between Article 100a and Article 118a (relating to health and safety at work), a conflict that is not easy to resolve.

The new approach: origins and principles

The Commission's new approach was designed to break the log-jam caused by the old-approach directives and to contain the development of national technical barriers that did not reflect European standards. The new approach was built on the information directive, proposed in 1980 and adopted in 1983, and took its essential structure from the precedents set by both the Low Voltage Directive (LVD) and the jurisprudence of the *Cassis de Dijon* case, which provided the definition for essential safety requirements. The aim of the information directive was to prevent the introduction of new technical barriers, both mandatory technical regulations adopted by member-states and voluntary standards worked out by private standards institutes. The directive requires member-states to notify drafts to the Commission and the other member-states. This must be done by 31 January of each year, and is followed by a three-month period during which the drafts can be commented on. The notifying state must take these comments into account 'as far as possible'. If the Commission considers that common measures would be in the Community's interest, it can announce its intention to propose a directive on the matter, in which case the notified measure may not be adopted until at least a year after notification.

After this directive's entry into force, 766 drafts of technical regulations had been notified by the end of 1989. Of these, 268 (over a third) came from Germany, 150 from France, 77 from Denmark and 69 from Britain.[2] In some cases the drafts were blocked by the introduction of Community directives and, in one-third of the cases, the draft initially notified was subsequently amended. It is the member-states that have to enforce the standstill on any national standards activity which is the subject of a Commission mandate to CEN/CENELEC. Failure to respect this obligation would amount to an infringement of Community law. All national standard work has to be notified to CEN/CENELEC, which passes on the information to the Commission – 3,600 items were notified in 1987 alone.

It is worth noting that the three main standards institutions – DIN

(Germany), BSI (United Kingdom) and AFNOR (France) – had already been exchanging their draft standards for mutual comment for many years. Discussion within this tripartite group remains very important, covering such subjects as drafts of new-approach directives and questions about the implementation of those already adopted. The Commission takes part in the meetings, and favours this trilateral approach, just as it in general favours bilateral exchanges in the technical sector.

The LVD had already introduced the concept of the delegation of competencies to standards institutions, but did not provide a detailed definition of the essential requirements to be met. The definition of 'essential safety requirements' stems from the *Cassis de Dijon* ruling. This approach (using a general reference to standards) stemmed from the German law of 1968 on the safety of equipment (*Gerätesicherheitsgesetz*). This contains a detailed list of standards which, although not strictly mandatory, have in practice had a quasi-compulsory character. The LVD approach spilled over the German border in the early 1980s, when the French exercised considerable political pressure against the profusion of DIN norms, which, they argued, aggravated their trade deficit with the Germans, particularly in the mechanical engineering sector. Subsequently, a list of technically equivalent French and German norms was published in the *Bundesanzeiger*, and five French test centres, which would be allowed to grant the GS label, were even specified in an annex to the *Gerätesicherheitsgesetz*.

The LVD set another precedent. When the directive was adopted in 1973, there were very few European standards to fill in the directive, but the standards of the International Electrotechnical Committee (IEC) did exist. Hence a large number of Harmonized Documents (HDs) could be adopted on the basis of such IEC standards. In the context of the LVD, the combination of general essential requirements and delegation of competence to the standard-making institutions was seen as introducing too great a freedom into the standards fields and allowing too much scope for safeguard clauses. Industrialists therefore took the initiative of pressing national certification bodies to come together within CENELEC in order to introduce some legal certainty. In the toys sectors, for example, British manufacturers had been striving for legal provisions rather than a voluntary standard. It is interesting that the same principle of 'reference to standard' was included in recommendations made by the UN Economic Commission for Europe since 1975, as well as in the 1980 GATT standard code.

A similar precedent for the EC's new approach can be found in British rules. British building regulations were amended in 1985 to include the concept of 'functional requirements', which corresponds closely to the Community phrase 'essential safety requirements'. The British also referred to 'guiding documents', which can be found in the EC's building-products directive. It was thus no coincidence that in the early 1980s the British government was one of the keenest advocates of what was to become the EC's new approach.

The new approach was fleshed out during the drafting of the old-approach pressure-vessel directive. For the first time, the distinction emerged between, on the one hand, essential requirements and, on the other, technical standards. The initiative stemmed as much from PNEUROP, the European trade association in this field, as from the Commission, but it was picked up and pushed forward by the Commission and some member-states, among which Britain was particularly active.

Each new-approach directive contains a set of core elements:

(1) the defined scope of the directive, as well as the products that it does *not* cover (e.g., sporting equipment is excluded from the toys directive);

(2) the essential requirements, formulated in terms of a 'general clause', since the legal text must itself provide judges with a sufficient basis for jurisprudence;

(3) methods of satisfying the essential requirements. Compliance with a European standard – a 'technical specification approved by a recognized standardized body for repeated or continuous application, with which compliance is not mandatory' (directive 83/189) – is simply the most convenient way of meeting the 'essential requirements', since the burden of proof is reversed (to the benefit of the manufacturer);

(4) safeguard procedures in the event of the detection of an unsafe product; and

(5) provisions about certification and methods of testing conformity with the essential requirements and procedures for affixing the EC mark.

The accumulation of Community jurisprudence has had a major impact on the removal of technical barriers. The *Dassonville* and *Cassis de Dijon* rulings, and their extension to similar cases on beer, pasta and milk, have been very efficient in removing barriers based on arbitrary discrimination against products from other member-states. Article 30

(EEC), which prohibits quantitative restrictions or 'measures with equivalent effect', has been invoked particularly successfully as regards barriers relating to the composition of products, especially foodstuffs and drinks. However, it has had less impact on barriers that result from different national provisions on health and safety, because, according to Article 36 (EEC), they represent permissible exceptions.[3]

Herein lies one of the key problems facing technical harmonization in the EC. How can a single EC market for products be achieved when it is still the member-states that have the ultimate responsibility for health and safety legislation? Moreover, consumer and environmental concerns have grown to an extent not foreseen when the Community was founded. Article 36 (EEC) does not even mention consumer protection, although in the *Cassis de Dijon* case the ECJ added it to the list of permissible exceptions.

Conformity assessment is one of the trickiest issues in the new approach. In July 1989, the Commission proposed a 'modular approach' in its long-awaited *Policy Statement on Technical Specifications, Testing and Certification – The Global Approach*. In December 1990, this was adopted in a revised form by a Council resolution, despite strong German objections.[4] The 'modules' would be used in subsequent new-approach directives and comprise the following elements: the design phase (module B: EC-type examination), the production stage (modules C-E: different types of EC declarations on production conformity, and module F: EC verification) and a combination of the two (module A: manufacturer's declaration of conformity, module G: EC verification, and module H: EC declaration of design and production conformity). The choice of conformity assessment procedures would depend partly on the required level of safety.

This module approach came out too late, and most of the new-approach directives had already been drafted. In the British case, the absence of a 'cross-directive' or horizontal approach to conformity assessment and certification had frequently been criticized, especially since the EC has sometimes adopted conflicting requirements under different directives. The Germans, on the other hand, were in favour of regulating conformity assessment in every directive, fearing that a modular approach might lead to a certain amount of unnecessary reregulation.

European standard-making
CEN and CENELEC were set up as individual entities towards the end of
the 1950s. The former was established in its present form in 1961, and the
latter in 1972. By analogy with IEC and ISO (International Standards
Organization), CENELEC is responsible for standardization in the
electrotechnical field, and CEN deals with all other sectors. Both are
private organizations established under Belgian law. In telecommunications there is a similar framework, with CEPT (European Conference of
Post and Telecommunications Authorities) and more recently ETSI (European Telecommunications Standards Institute) and the International Telecommunication Union's Consultative Committee on International Telex
and Telecommunications (CCITT).

Although some 1,250 European standards (ENs) have already been
worked out, national standards still exceed those at the European level by
nine to one. In Germany, for example, there were 20,000 DIN standards
in 1989. This compared with 9,400 ISO and IEC (i.e. international)
standards. The various interested parties still provide their inputs through
national channels, but, as yet, there is no organized European industrial
opinion. Participation is open to standards bodies from both EC and
EFTA countries, although it is very common for only a couple of
interested standard-making institutions to take part in the actual drafting
work within the technical committees. The main pressure-vessel standard, for instance, was worked out by Germany, France, Britain and
Austria. ENs are adopted by a qualified majority vote of the member
institutions.

The weighting of votes follows the rules for the EC Council (Article
148 EEC), with corresponding weighting for EFTA members. These
range from ten votes for the four big standard institutions, AFNOR, BSI,
DIN and UNI (Italy), to one vote for Iceland; there are 96 votes in all, 76
of which are from EC countries. For ENs to be adopted, four specific
requirements have to be met: (1) simple majority (without abstentions);
(2) at least 25 weighted votes in favour; (3) no more than 22 weighted
votes against; and (4) no more than three members against the proposal.

If the proposed standard fails to meet these requirements, a second
counting is held, excluding non-EC members. This is rare, but it did
prove necessary for the adoption of Part III of the toys standards (EN
71-3), relating to their chemical properties. Four countries had voted
against the proposal (Britain, Germany, Belgium and Austria), and the
Netherlands had abstained. In the second counting, EN 71-3 was adopted
in spite of the opposition of Britain and Germany, the latter having also

voted against EN 71-1 (covering mechanical and physical properties).

Since 1985, an adopted EN has had to be implemented in full as a national standard by all EC standards institutions, regardless of the way in which the individual member voted, and it thus replaces any previous national standard in conflict with the EN. EFTA countries, by contrast, are obliged to introduce the EN nationally only if they voted in favour of it. Therefore, in the toys case (EN 71-3), all EFTA countries except Austria had to implement the standard. Compliance with this obligation to implement is in practice more regular than is the case for EC legislation under Article 169 (EEC) procedures.

Where ENs are intended to complete an EC directive, the Commission gives a precise mandate to CEN or CENELEC, with a (usually extremely tight) deadline and financial provisions. Roughly 70% of the costs are borne by the national standard institutes: in 1988 DIN provided about 27% (32% in 1986/87), AFNOR 17% (27%), BSI 17% (15%), and the other member-states contributed 39%. Contributions from EC bodies provide 86% of total funding, with the remaining 14% coming from EFTA-based bodies. EFTA countries give a separate mandate and funds to CEN/CENELEC for those standards that its members wish to join.

For each standard, a secretariat is provided by one of the national standard bodies. The question of how many secretariats are held by each national organization has often had highly political overtones, and been a subject of particular concern in Britain. The aim of every government seems to have been to make sure that its standard-making body provides as many secretariats as possible. Although control of the secretariat can help to influence the work and, particularly, the pace of standard-making, this should not be over-estimated. In March 1989, Germany's DIN/DKE held 75 out of 212 CEN/CENELEC secretariats for technical committees, i.e. 35.4%. The British BSI held 18.4% (its share having grown in recent years) and the French AFNOR/UTE, 17.9% (see Tables 4.1 and 4.2). The technical board of CEN allocates the secretariats, very often to the national institute that has submitted a proposal or that already provides the relevant ISO secretariat. A purely quantitative assessment is, therefore, extremely misleading. The DIN retains from a previous period many secretariats whose scope is limited compared with that of many of the more recent secretariats, which cover very broad fields with far higher economic importance.

Our interviews suggest that cooperation and harmonization between the Commission and the European standards institutions are still perceived as being too unidirectional. CEN/CENELEC apparently do not

Table 4.1 Distribution of secretariats in CEN/CENELEC (March 1989)

	CEN	ECISS	CENELEC	CEN/CENELEC Total
Number of technical committees	141	23	48	212
Secretariats held by DIN/DKE	52	5	18	75 (35.4%)
Secretariats held by BSI	· 29	2	8	39 (18.4%)
Secretariats held by AFNOR/UTE	24	5	9	38 (17.9%)

Source: Deutsche Industrie-Normen.

receive enough feedback from the Commission and are often subjected to deadlines that are considered too tight and in some cases unrealistic. The scope for standardization under the rubric of some new-approach directives (e.g. machinery safety) is so large that a programming committee has had to be set up to establish consistency.[5]

EC-wide representation of interests is still a tricky issue. Several attempts have been made, notably by trade unions and consumer associations, to secure seats in CEN/CENELEC committees. An alternative is for consumers to seek to influence standard-making by persuading national delegations to vote for the consumer position – after all, if more than three members vote against a proposal it fails. Such a reliance on national representation is consistent with the established practice in standard-making. The alternative EC-level representation raises the real problem of how to determine who is an 'interested European party'. There is, none the less, a lack of consumer and trade union involvement, particularly in the South European countries. In the short-to-medium term, the best remedy probably lies in an improvement of the standard-making processes within member-states, and a different division of labour between public agencies and private standards bodies – the Portuguese Standards Institute is, for example, still part of the Ministry of Industrial Affairs. (For the status of the different standard-making bodies see Table 4.2.)

Table 4.2 European standard-making bodies

Country	Body	Status[1]	Staff	No. of pages of standards[2]	Approx. no. of standards per year	CEN secre-tariats 1987[3]
FRG	DIN	b	596	120,000 (20,500)	1,400	34
DK	DS	a	65	15,000 (2,355)	250	6
E	AENOR	a	70	78,200 (6,589)	850	0
F	AFNOR	a	446	138,344 (13,366)	1,100	17
I	UNI	a	48	30,000 (6,411)	270	3
NL	NNI	b	100	55,000 (5,500)	110	2
UK	BSI	a	1,200[4]	125,000 (9,360)	660	10

Source: Florence Nicolas and Jacques Repussard, *Common Standards for Firms*, Commission of the European Communities, Brussels, 1988, p. 26, based on ISO and CEN documents for 1986.

[1] (a) Private organization, but recognized also for public tasks; (b) Private organization.
[2] Approximate number of standards in parentheses.
[3] Applies to only 82 technical committees, hence the figures do not correspond to those in Table 4.1.
[4] Half deal with testing and certification.

Differences between Germany and Britain

The principles underlying the new approach are well understood and supported in both Britain and Germany. Our interview results suggest that when it comes to the detailed work on directives, differences often reflect the different personalities involved, rather than different national approaches.

In principle, a deregulatory approach is followed in both countries. In Germany, however, one of the hypotheses that we set out to test, and proved to be correct, was that the search for consensus is much more important than in Britain and should be considered fundamental to the economic architecture of the German state. It is long-established practice for employers and unions to work together in formulating regulations (notably within the framework of the craft guilds) and to favour European-level harmonization in order to protect themselves against 'unlawful competition' from other countries. This adds a regulatory bias, reinforced by the role of organized consumer interests, perhaps as a result of their deep-rooted links to the trade union movement. This tradition of involving the social patterns in making standards is not found in Britain, where the emphasis is instead on involving companies with relevant knowledge and interests.

Overall, there is a stronger 'standards reflex' in Germany than in any other EC country. The number of established standards is certainly large, although not significantly larger than elsewhere in the EC; and the number of pages of standards issued is actually in line with that of other large member-states, including Britain (see Table 4.2). The figures are somewhat misleading because DIN often produces several standards, where elsewhere there is only one. Once a standard has been established, there is an impressive level of compliance in Germany in contrast with some other member-states, where standards are less readily accepted by users and producers alike. This problem predates the adoption of the new approach.

Lack of compliance can have ironic consequences. In the pre-Christmas 1988 season, the French authorities decided to limit the sale of imported, mostly Japanese, toys in France, by transforming a voluntary French standard on electronic toys into a mandatory regulation. It turned out that the only manufacturers which could and already did produce to the French standard were not the French but the Japanese.

There are some interesting variations of approach to standard-making that are at odds with the general national approaches to 1992. Contrary to the normal non-interventionist/voluntarist approach in Britain, it was considered necessary to have an active DTI campaign in order to encourage more company involvement in the standard-making processes. In contrast, the German approach is almost exclusively determined by DIN with no government involvement. Whereas in Britain the DTI has doubled the number of staff working on the standards dimension of 1992, the German Ministry of Economics has made no changes in its standards unit; and it is DIN that has created a European unit specifically to handle the new approach. Within the BSI, there have also been moves to coordinate work on 1992 issues, but the bulk of the information work, and much of the initiative for change, came out of the DTI.

A major Anglo-German contrast can be found in the accreditation systems used in each country. In Britain there is a centralized system, but as yet nothing of the kind exists in Germany, where most certification bodies are private, even if, like the technical approval associations (TüVs), they partly perform public functions, such as those under paragraph 24 of the trading law (*Gewerbeordnung*). The European Commission favours centralized accreditation systems of the British kind for both test houses and certification bodies. The Germans are predictably not keen on such developments, which they consider lead to unnecessary regulation.

Britain has hardly any mandatory third-party certification, preferring instead to ensure a high level of quality by emphasizing quality assurance systems. Although based on a set of common procedural rules set out in EN 29.000 (BS 5750), quality assurance gives considerable flexibility to individual companies. In contrast, quality assurance is used in Germany for only a very limited number of especially critical products. Germans tend to regard Britain's emphasis on quality assurance as being a result of efforts to correct previously poor levels of product quality, which were having an adverse effect on British competitiveness. The Commission has, with its more recent initiatives, moved towards the British approach, supporting third-party certified quality assurance systems. Examples include the modification of the directive on personal protective equipment and active implantable medical instruments, e.g. pacemakers, both of which have been adopted, as well as the changes made in the 'global approach'. Wherever possible, Germans tend to favour self-certification by manufacturers. If this is inappropriate, the second German option is type-approval, and only then the quality assurance route, sometimes on the basis of second-party certification.

As for the operations of the two standards institutes, two major differences distinguish the BSI and DIN: their financing and the way they handle drafts for public comment. The BSI receives only general membership fees from its members and does not charge for participation in the specific technical committees (TCs) that discuss standards. Within DIN, the members of a TC will often provide most of its funding. Such contributions account for 11% of DIN resources, compared with 8% from general membership, 19% from government funding, and the remainder (62%) from publications and other activities. The British sometimes argue that this German practice could compromise the independence of the standard-making procedures. On the other hand, the German government has always allocated public funds to standard-making activities, a system introduced only recently in Britain. (Such funds increased by 64% between 1985 and 1988 in Britain.) Under the earlier 'pound-for-pound' grant system in Britain, there was no attempt by the DTI to set priorities in standard-making within the BSI. The other main difference is that when a draft standard is published for public comment, the BSI is not obliged to hold a formal hearing with those who wish to make comments. In DIN (and AFNOR), all those who wish to must be given a formal opportunity to present their case.

Third-party certification is not frequently used in either country. This is contrary to the generally held belief that third-party certification is widely used in Germany. It is in fact limited (under paragraph 24 of the trading law) to certain installations that are considered potentially dangerous, such as pressure vessels. Steps have also been taken to move away from such mandatory third-party certification in domestic German law in order to deregulate, as has been the case with lifts. Within the FRG, the Federal and Länder governments have different views on this issue. At the Federal level, there is a reluctance to use third-party certification. On the other hand, the Länder governments, which have considerable powers under paragraph 24 of the trading law, strongly favour it because it facilitates enforcement, for which they are responsible.

A comparison of Britain and Germany must also take account of the important differences in basic philosophies, such as the contrast between common and Roman law, or the differing attitudes to safety procedures. As regard fire hazards, for instance, the Germans have long stressed the importance of escape routes, whereas the British put the accent on the actual fire prevention. The Germans have thus been puzzled by some British requirements, such as the insistence that children's nightwear must be 100% fireproof.

The Länder dimension in Germany deserves particular attention. There is a tradition of conflict between the Länder enforcement authorities and Federal regulators, which has a parallel in Britain in tensions between central government regulation and local enforcement authorities. However, in the context of the new-approach directives, other Federal/Länder divergences arise. The building-products directive, for example, raises a particular problem by touching on an area of exclusive Länder competence. The German law of 19 December 1986, ratifying the Single European Act, stipulates that when EC regulations touch upon laws and regulations of the Länder, the Federal government must consider the position of the Federal Council (Bundesrat) and may diverge from this position only if there are 'essential foreign or integration policy reasons' for so doing. The Länder government is particularly worried that it has no direct representation in the standing committee set up to deal with enforcement of the building-products directive. This Committee has two representatives per country and will exercise important regulatory powers.

Has the new approach lived up to the expectations?

The first question is whether the new-approach directives have in practice respected the principles underlying the concept. Limiting the directives to establishing 'essential safety requirements' implies entirely new working methods and a very different approach on the part of public authorities. This endeavour has just about succeeded, in that technical details within the directives have been kept to a minimum. There are, however, some anomalies carried over from early efforts at harmonization. For example, Annex II of the toys directive does not have the intended general clause to establish minimum requirements, instead it contains the remains of earlier drafts, dealing with aspects that should really have been incorporated in the form of a standard. There is still a tendency for national delegations to increase, arbitrarily, this or that quantitative legal requirement of a standard under the pretext of seeking to achieve a higher degree of safety. Interviewees also claimed that the technical specifications set out in the legislative texts contained some simple errors, probably stemming from a lack of technical expertise on the part of the negotiators or from the political imperative of making a compromise in order to get a directive through. According to those interviewed, such simple technical errors were incorporated in the toys and pressure-vessels directives, for example. The legal status of the directives prevent them being easily corrected.

Even when the new approach works as it should, there is a tendency not only to delegate to the standard-making bodies, but also to defer problems to a later stage, and to pass the buck from the legislators to the standard-makers. A standing committee, such as the one created by the building-products directive, can then become a 'dustbin' for all the questions that could not be solved during the negotiation of the directive. Such problems derive partly from the considerable time pressures imposed by each EC Council presidency in its desire to adopt as many internal-market directives as possible. This often leads the Council to grant important regulatory powers to standing committees, a development that the Commission does not favour at all.

There is also a tremendous overlap between the competencies of national ministries and Commission DGs, and inconsistencies between their strategies. Such overlaps affect not only the negotiation, but also the implementation of the directives. Inconsistencies can also be found between directives, both between the old- and the new-approach directives and among those based on the new approach.

So far, as explained above, the issue of certification and conformity assessment has been treated separately in every directive. The German approach was to keep the directive as self-contained as possible, as with the building-products directive, whereas Britain kept asking for a more horizontal approach. Hence there are logical inconsistencies between, for example, the proposal for the protective-equipment directive, which relies heavily on type-approval for comparatively straightforward products, and the machinery-safety directive, under which far more dangerous products do not require such type-approval. Similar inconsistencies can be found between the lifting-machinery directive and earlier ones covering passenger lifts or industrial trucks. Moreover, type-approval systems differ from one directive to another, with the result that the wheel is constantly being reinvented.

Serious difficulties arise from the extent to which different EC directives cover the same products. The LVD is the most severe case. It is estimated that roughly 80% of the products covered by the machinery-safety directive have to meet conflicting requirements under the LVD, such as the existence or non-existence of the EC mark. Electrical wood-working machines, regulated in Annex IV of the machinery-safety directive, are subject to particularly difficult conflicts of requirements.

Some of these difficulties stem from inadequate coordination within the Commission between DG III, involved in all Article 100a directives under the new approach, and DG V, responsible for the drafting of Article 118a (health and safety) directives. The two DGs sometimes even seem to have a competitive, rather than a cooperative, relationship. Particularly as regards the machinery-safety directives, the distinction between trade-related aspects (including a number of technical specifications) and social or political questions related to the work place has been handled in a manner that is far from satisfactory, with DG V sometimes duplicating the work of DG III.

Similar problems are evident at the national level, since each ministry has its own approach. In Germany, for example, the Federal Ministry of Labour and Social Affairs took the lead for the directives on pressure vessels, toys and machinery safety, although the directives were taken through the Internal Market Council – in which the Federal Ministry of

Economics usually leads – and not the Social Affairs Council of the EC. Before the common EC position for the machinery-safety directive was reached in December 1988, views diverged between the Federal Ministry of Economics, which favoured the directive on the grounds of its trade-liberating effects, and the Federal Ministry of Labour and Social Affairs, which was far more concerned with the enforcement difficulties. The latter particularly opposed the provisions of Article 5 for the transitional period, and supported, like the European Parliament, enhanced obligations for third-party certification. In the end, Germany was the only member-state to vote against the directive in the Council; the Ministry of Economics ultimately adopted the Ministry of Labour's reservations. This negative vote should probably be seen as a political gesture to the Ministry of Labour, since an EC majority was always going to override the German reservations. But also, according to the EC Commission's interpretation of the Single European Act, a member-state can invoke Article 100a.4 (i.e., the possibility of applying higher national requirements) only if it voted against the directive.

The main practical problems for the new approach are whether the essential safety requirements of all the relevant directives will be complete by 1992, and what will happen if they are not. In the cases we have examined, whereas ENs for toys and pressure vessels either have already been adopted or are well advanced, it seems highly unlikely that sufficient standards for the directives on machinery safety and building products will be agreed. The first new-approach directive on pressure vessels, however, entered into force on 1 July 1990 without all the necessary standards having been adopted. One of the problems with the building-products directive is that the essential safety requirements refer to the actual buildings, whereas standards will have to be worked out for the construction products as well. For the machinery-safety directive alone it is estimated that 200–300 ENs are needed. CEN will probably be given an open-ended mandate, but will still be faced with a huge challenge.

There is therefore considerable pressure on the European standards institutions to work out the necessary ENs quickly. The introduction of qualified majority voting has already helped to speed things up, as has the reorientation of industry (traditionally favouring national or international standardization) towards taking a much stronger interest in ENs. But further attention must be given to the question of how to meet the essential safety requirements if relevant standards are not agreed. If standards are formulated too vaguely, the lack of legal certainty can also result in a rush to get them agreed, which in turn risks regular recourse to safeguard clauses.

It is not possible, however, to make the entry into force of the directives dependent upon the existence of the necessary ENs. This would create constitutional problems, because legislative powers would effectively be ceded to the standards institutions. One must also bear in mind that it should be possible to change standards in the event of technical progress.

Conclusion

The introduction of the new approach to standard-making in the EC has introduced a deregulatory bias. The stress laid on the formulation of essential requirements in the directives is clearly an attempt to regulate only what is absolutely necessary at the European level and to apply the principle of subsidiarity. However, there is some evidence that this approach contains an intrinsic danger in that difficult decisions are sometimes pushed into the standard-making process, rather than being faced at the time directives are negotiated. Whatever happens, the political will shown in agreeing on the directives will have to be matched by an even greater effort on the standards front.

Moreover, our interviews with decision-makers on standards have revealed that the respective British and German approaches are far less clear-cut with regard to technical harmonization than the general comparison of national approaches might suggest. Paradoxically, the Germans seem to fear that EC legislation, influenced by the British approach to, for example, third-party certification of quality assurance systems, may lead to excessive regulation. This case-study has also shown the tremendous practical role that inconspicuous sub-structures, and sub-networks and technical committees in the area of standardization, play in the quest to complete the single market.

5

TELECOMMUNICATIONS

The significance of the telecommunications sector

The telecommunications sector is of especial interest because it embodies most of the significant policy areas affected by 1992: standards; testing and certification; public procurement; competition, and mergers and acquisitions; and deregulation and re-regulation. The Community's telecommunications policies have three interconnected (but not necessarily convergent) objectives:

(1) to establish a coherent and effective telecommunications infrastructure for the EC;

(2) to promote competition and improve the range and quality of telecommunications services; and

(3) to promote the development and global competitiveness of the EC's telecommunications equipment manufacturers.

The importance of telecommunications to every sector of the economy is obvious, and the objectives of the EC's 1987 Green Paper, *The Development of the Common Market for Telecommunications Services and Equipment*, are among the most ambitious of all the 1992-related initiatives. However, some have argued that current changes – in the structure of the industry, in trade patterns and in the regulatory environment – are more the product of rapid technological change than a result of the deregulatory climate of the 1980s.[1]

Even if the changes are technology-driven, however, the question of what constitutes the appropriate regulatory environment is a central

58

issue. Given the immense economic, social and strategic importance of telecommunications, total deregulation is hardly possible, the market must be administered to some degree at both the national and the EC level. There is therefore likely to be increasing pressures for *liberalization*, but not necessarily for *deregulation*, in the sense of a net reduction in regulation (whether carried out at the member-state or Community level).

The EC market for telecommunications services is one of its largest and most dynamic sectors – worth around 80bn ecus (1988 figures) and projected to grow at an annual rate of 11.5% to 154bn ecus by 1995. This is two to three times the projected real rate of growth of the European economies as a whole. Four main markets account for over 82% of revenues and 76% of the Community's 125 million telephone lines: Germany (24% of total revenues, 27m lines); France (22%, 26m); UK (22%, 23m); Italy (14%, 19m). Over 60% of telecommunications revenues come from business customers; and 52% of 1988 revenues were derived from trunk and international calls, as against 20% from local calls.

Although there has for some years been an appreciable element of competition in the United Kingdom (notably in cellular services and customer equipment, and of course the British Telecom/Mercury network duopoly), services in the rest of the Community are provided under monopoly legislation by state PTT organizations (Germany, France, Belgium and Luxembourg), corporations wholly owned by PTTs or local authorities (Netherlands, Ireland, Greece, Italy and Denmark), or public companies in which effective control is exercised by the state (Spain and Portugal). One consequence of this political control has been the incorporation into the responsibilities of the Public Telecommunication Organizations (PTO) of a range of social costs, such as the principle of uniform charges for services (*Tarifeinheit*) and country-wide coverage (*Flächenversorgung*).

The different objectives established for each country's service provider has meant that tariffs vary widely, with a general pattern of long-distance services cross-subsidizing local services. Calling Spain from Germany costs 41% of the rate charged to call Germany from Spain; in the United Kingdom trunk calls are 2.7 times more expensive than local calls, while in Germany they are 15.1 times more expensive; new-subscriber connection charges cost 150 ecus in the United Kingdom, and 31 ecus in Germany.

The telecommunications administrations in the EC are responsible for over 70% of telecommunications equipment purchases, with no member-state accounting for more than 6% of the world telecommunications market (compared with 35% for the United States and 11% for Japan).[2] The establishment of comprehensive national networks led to close cooperation between national telecommunications administrations and their suppliers, often with different network technology and standards. This has resulted in a fragmented industrial structure in the sector, with little cross-border trade.

In 1988, mobile communications, ISDN, and data and text services accounted for less than 10% of total revenues. Forecasts indicate that these same services will account for nearly half the market in 1995. The transformation of the sector is only partly the result of public-policy initiatives, such as the EC Commission's Green Paper or the changes in the regulatory regimes in the United Kingdom and, more recently, in other member-states. The moves towards competitive services are driven by changes in network technology (digitization, optoelectronics and satellite communication), rising customer demand for cheaper and more sophisticated voice, data and text services, and a change in political attitudes, which are now less inclined to defend inefficient and unresponsive public-sector monopolies.

The structure of the telecommunications equipment industry

The major companies in the European telecommunications equipment industry (with the partial exception of Philips and Ericsson) are heavily dependent on the European market, and in most cases even this European element is attributable largely to home-market, rather than cross-border, sales; the failure to open up public procurement in telecommunications is, of course, the main reason for this.

The escalating cost and shortening life-cycle of new products have meant that not even the 'national champions' can now remain viable without substantial sales outside their home market. Whereas twenty years ago an electromechanical switching system would cost 15-20m ecus to develop and could be expected to last, substantially unmodified, for 20-30 years, a digital switching system now costs up to 1bn ecus to develop and has a life-cycle of no more than 10 years, and then only with continuous updating of its software.

Firms producing such digital public-switching systems would therefore need to gain an 8% world-market share in order to break even, but even the largest national telecommunications market in the Community represents less than 6% of the world market.[3] North American firms currently sell four rival digital-switching systems, Japanese companies have three, and European manufacturers, no less than six. Given that each system costs 1bn ecus to develop, all six European manufacturers would have to divide the entire world market between them in order to produce the next generation of switches.[4] This means that the EC market, which represents approximately a quarter of the world market, can probably support only two or three systems developers, who would be either multinational consortia or the product of mergers and acquisitions. Clear signs of the pressure to restructure the industry can be seen in the GEC-Siemens takeover of Plessey in 1989, and the Siemens acquisition of Nixdorf in 1990.

The equipment manufacturers have been forced to seek export markets to expand their sales, but the liberalization of telecommunications equipment procurement (notably the freeing of the terminal-equipment market) in Europe has increased competition at home and abroad. Liberalization has made the European telecommunications market very attractive to American and Japanese firms, which are likewise anxious to cover their escalating R&D costs; the Community has a trade deficit with the United States and Japan for every category of telecommunications equipment, and even France and Germany (the only countries not in overall deficit) have a positive balance only in the switching equipment category.[5]

Although there were approximately 1,000 firms in the EC making telecommunications equipment in mid-1988, representing 31% of world production, the sector is dominated by the major pan-European firms (Alcatel, Siemens, Ericsson, Philips). The smaller national champions (GPT, Bosch, Italtel) have significant shares of their home markets, but not of other EC markets. The sector as a whole is fairly concentrated – the top seven European firms together account for over 80% of telecommunications equipment sales in Europe – and not very profitable, with profits standing at about 3% of turnover, according to one estimate.[6] In 1990, facing a sharp drop in profitability, Philips withdrew from its equipment-manufacturing joint venture with AT&T, and was seen by some industry analysts as likely to exit from the telecommunications business altogether.[7]

The regulatory environment in Britain and Germany

The restructuring of the telecommunications service industry and its regulatory environment has also accelerated in the past five years. This has gone furthest in the United Kingdom, with the separation of the British Post Office from telecommmunications services in 1981, followed by the privatization of British Telecom in 1984 (and the licensing of Mercury as a competing operator in the public telecommunications network) under the supervision of Oftel as an independent regulator. There is also competition in mobile radio telephony – between two consortia – and three multinational consortia are establishing more limited personal communications networks. In 1989, the British DTI decided to implement an Oftel proposal permitting private network operators to share or sell capacity to third parties, including voice-telephony service. The following year, the British government announced that it would end the BT/Mercury duopoly in voice telephony and permit third parties to enter the sector and interconnect with existing subscriber networks.

Overall, the United Kingdom is the most liberalized telecommunications market in Europe; it is the first EC member-state to separate the provision and the regulation of telecommunications services. However, the process has been one of structured and regulated liberalization. This is shown by the guarantee of an initial duopoly in voice telecommunications, instituted to protect BT's much smaller competitor Mercury from third-party ventures, and by the prevention of British Telecom and Mercury from moving into cable television. Competition and market access have been consciously limited in the United Kingdom in order to ensure that British Telecom's dominant position does not prevent the development of effective competitors. Although in 1984 the British government did not opt to break up British Telecom along the lines of the AT&T divestiture in the United States, the 1990 review of the duopoly seemed set on replacing it with free competition in telecommunications (subject to certain service obligations and access charges), with telephone subscribers gaining equal access to rival operators through network interconnection.[8]

In Germany, the high costs of telecommunications services (private circuits, for example, cost at least four times as much as in the United Kingdom) led to pressures in the 1980s from German business for the introduction of greater competition and the separation of the Deutsche Bundespost's service provision and regulatory functions. In September 1987, the Witte Commission reported on future regulation of the sector, resulting in the introduction in March 1988 of draft legislation, the *Poststrukturgesetz*, to establish Deutsche Bundespost Telekom as a public enterprise. The measure was passed by the Bundestag in April 1989 and came into effect on 1 July 1989. Its three key points are:

(1) division of the DBP into three businesses (Telekom, Postdienst and Postbank), with regulation and equipment type-approval by the Federal Ministry of Posts and Telecommunications;[9]

(2) continuation of the DBP monopoly over the network and voice-telephony service (which earns 90% of telecommunications income) in order to ensure mandatory nationwide service provision and tariff uniformity, with competition in fringe areas, such as low-power satellite systems, radio-paging and mobile-radio networks, and free competition – in which Telekom may participate – in all value-added services; and

(3) complete freedom in the terminal-equipment supply market.

The new law does not incorporate the Witte Commission's recommendation that Telekom's network monopoly be reviewed every three years, and, despite pressure from telecommunications users in Germany, there has been no move towards establishing a duopoly based on the British model. There is also a substantial grey area in the regulation of cross-subsidies, in which the Federal government has said that 'financial surpluses of the monopoly services can be used to compensate for the additional costs or revenue losses that result from Telekom's infrastructural obligations in the competitive area'.[10] Overall, the implementation of the 1989 law appears to steer a middle course between the liberalization model adopted by the United Kingdom and the status quo wanted by the Deutsche Postgewerkschaft, the DBP workers' union. It should be noted that the German Basic Law forbids privatization of the telephone network, and a constitutional amendment would require a two-thirds majority in the Bundestag – a difficult objective, since the Social Democrat Party (SPD) opposes privatization.

In some respects, however, the new telecommunications regime in Germany is even more liberal than that in the United Kingdom. There are no licensing restrictions on entry into the value-added-services market, for example, and shared use and resale of international leased circuits is generally permitted. In July 1990 (partly in response to the need to establish adequate telecommunications links between East and West Germany prior to unification) the DBP introduced the most liberal satellite communications policy in the EC, in the shape of a new licensing scheme permitting interactive satellite networks, including provision of voice telephony. It could be argued that, aside from the network monopoly, there is no inherent obstacle in Germany to further liberalization, and that DBP Telekom's dominant position will inevitably be eroded as new technologies and services are introduced. Indeed, the special problems posed by German unification in 1990 (there were only 800 lines between East and West at the beginning of the year, rising to 2,600 at the end) caused Telekom to suspend its voice-telephony monopoly for three years to permit private satellite links into the five Eastern Länder; Post Minister Christian Schwarz-Schilling even raised the possibility that minority capital participation in Telekom by outsiders might be necessary to help overcome the fiscal and technical obstacles to recabling East Germany.[11]

EC initiatives in telecommunications

In the mid-1990s, thanks to a number of convergent developments, the Commission was presented with an opportunity to move forward in its attempt to formulate a Community strategy for telecommunications. Some progress had already been made in the areas of prior notification of new national standards (1983), the new approach to technical harmonization and rule-setting (1985), and the mutual recognition of type-approval for terminal equipment (1986). The Commission had also proposed opening up public procurement in the telecommunications sector and had persuaded the Council to launch the full-scale RACE programme to develop hardware and software for broad-band communications networks. What remained untouched, however, was the whole question of regulatory reform and the creation of an open market in telecommunications services.

In many respects, circumstances favoured a Commission initiative in telecommunications. The first stimulus for change is that, although the EC is still competitive with Japan and the United States in switching and networks, it lags behind them in microelectronics and computing – the technologies that will be crucial for the next generation of telecommunications networks. Technological imperatives therefore mandated change in both the industrial and the market structures of the EC. The second stimulus for change is that the telematics era represents the merging of the telecommunications sector, which is by tradition heavily-regulated, with the totally unregulated computer market, and existing regulatory regimes are neither appropriate nor adaptable. Therefore, in all the member-states, the question of deregulation and reregulation of telecommunications was on the agenda.

There were thus strong incentives for the Commission to try to guide the reassessment these developments were causing in all the member-states, lest the inevitable liberalization at the national level create divergent and incompatible telecommunications structures that would prevent or delay the creation of a single market. The Green Paper of June 1987 placed the Commission firmly in the liberal camp, favouring the abolition of monopolies for the supply of all terminal and network equipment and value-added services, while retaining PTT monopolies only in the provision of basic telephone services. The Green Paper also advocated the clear separation of the regulatory and operations functions of PTTs, the recognition that tariffs should be responsive to cost trends (notably the falling cost of long-distance calls), and the promotion of balanced development, including the outlying regions. In addition, it called for the establishment of common European positions in international bodies, such as GATT and the International Telecommunications Union (ITU), and the creation of a European Standards Institute, staffed by experts and seconded by network operators and industry.

The Commission's strategy was to build up momentum for change even at the expense of clarity and coherence. The Green Paper's definition of the basic services that were to remain the exclusive preserve of PTTs, for example, left open the possibility of extending these beyond voice telephony, and the policy choice of flat versus variable tariffs remained fudged. But, at the same time, it made it clear that there were sufficient powers in the EEC Treaty and the ECJ decisions for the single market in telecommunications to be built.

In view of a later controversy concerning the Commission's use of Article 90(3) (EEC) instead of Article 100a (EEC) in its terminal equipment and services directives (see below), it is interesting to note that the Green Paper even made explicit reference to the *British Telecom* case, in which the ECJ ruled that PTTs were subject to Community competition law, since they supply goods and services for payment, which can be regarded as commercial undertakings.[12] To this extent, the Commission was talking softly, but letting everyone know that a big stick was at hand.

The response to the Green Paper

As it turned out, in the following six months DG XIII (the directorate-general responsible for telecommunications) received 61 submissions on the Green Paper proposals, ranging from the American Chamber of Commerce in Belgium to the VDMA (German Machinery and Equipment Manufacturers). All but a handful were supportive of the overall thrust of the Green Paper – the most negative came from the German

Postal Users' Association, which considered that the Green Paper's proposals would lead to over-regulation and negate the benefits of liberalization. In addition to the parallel discussions within the Senior Official Groups on telecommunications (SOG-T), the response to the Green Paper represented the most wide-ranging consultation the Community has ever undertaken in the telecommunications field.

The responses revealed broad support for liberalization in terminal equipment and value-added services, full endorsement of the separation of PTT regulation and network operation, and strong support for common standards to facilitate inter-operability and open-network provision. Some proposals, such as the exclusive PTT provision-of-network infrastructure and voice-telephony services, were variously criticized both for going too far and for not going far enough. On some other issues, such as satellite communications, multilateral negotiations, regional development and the social impact of the proposals, there was either little expressed interest or no clear convergence of opinion.

In February 1988, as a result of this consultation, the Commission approved its framework for further action, outlined in the document 'Implementing the Green Paper' (COM/88/48), which remains the blueprint for its current programme in telecommunications. This left for later initiatives other topics touched on in the Green Paper, such as the future regulation and development of satellite communications, and aimed, in essence, to implement the following measures to open the Community's telecommunications market:

(1)   liberalization of the terminal-equipment market and full mutual recognition of type-approval;
(2)   opening of the telecommunications-services market to competition;
(3)   separation of regulatory and operational functions of PTTs;
(4)   open-network provision;
(5)   opening up public procurement in telecommunications;
(6)   establishment of a European Telecommunications Standards Institute.

Implementing the Green Paper
At its meeting on 30 June 1988, the Telecommunications Council adopted a resolution that gave general support to the Commission's programme. This represented a hard-fought consensus position, in which the United Kingdom and Germany formed the core of the pro-liberalization

group, backed in most respects by the Dutch and the Danes. The existence of this core group and the passage of the Council resolution were
important because they ensured at the outset that both the Commission
and the Council were publicly committed to a certain degree of liberalization, and it was clear from the initial positions taken by member-states
that a blocking minority existed in the Council to prevent illiberal
measures from being introduced.

Six weeks earlier, the Commission had adopted the 'Directive on
competition in the markets in telecommunications terminal equipment'.[13]
Despite its issuance under Article 90(3) of the EEC Treaty, the directive
did not undermine the Council's consensus. The directive established a
timetable for removing the PTTs' exclusive rights to sell, instal and
maintain various types of terminal equipment, and obliges them to
publish the specifications for access to their networks. Although the
member-states generally supported the substance of the directive, considerable controversy was caused by the use of Article 90(3) (EEC),
which the Commission considers gives it the power to act against state
monopolies that are infringing the Community's rules on competition
and does not require Council approval. On 22 July 1988, France challenged the directive before the ECJ, arguing that Article 90 does not give
the Commission an absolute power to abolish monopolies; Germany,
Italy and Belgium have also joined the action, but the United Kingdom –
despite being unhappy about the means employed to achieve an end it
much desired – stood aside.

Although the Court is not due to issue a judgment on this case until
some time in early 1991, in February 1990 an advocate-general to the
ECJ delivered an opinion (not binding on the judges) that the Commission should use Article 90(3) (EEC) only for particular infringements by
individual member-states, and not for general legislative measures –
inherently a much more protracted process. The terminal-equipment
directive meanwhile remains in force. Given that all twelve telecommunications administrations publically supported the objective of the directive, these implementation problems do not augur well for the more
contentious services-directive discussed below.

Closely connected with the terminal-equipment directive is the draft
proposal for a 'Council directive on the mutual recognition of type-
approval for telecommunications terminal equipment'. Since this directive is based on Article 100a (EEC), it has not aroused as much controversy, although a large number of user and manufacturer groups have
lobbied against the draft directive's broad definition of terminal equip-

ment, which they contend could include every item of equipment attached to a private network or distributed computer system. These groups argue that instead of speeding up the approvals process, the draft directive might add unnecessary costs, limit consumer choice and delay introduction of new equipment because of its overprotectiveness in the attempt to guarantee network integrity. In June 1990, as a result of these representations, the Telecommunications Council achieved a common position on the requirement for type-approval, limiting it to terminal equipment used on public networks (not private networks) for the reserved services of voice and telex.[14] After amendments from the European Parliament have been considered by the Commission, adoption will probably take place in early 1991.

In December 1988, the Commission tabled for discussion a 'Draft directive on competition in the markets for telecommunications services', again under Article 90(3) (EEC). If anything, this was even more controversial than the other Article 90(3) directive on terminal equipment, in that only Germany and the United Kingdom fully supported the substance of the measure, which required member-states to remove exclusive rights for the supply of telecommunications services other than voice telephony. The Netherlands and Denmark added limited support for the Anglo-German position, thus forming a blocking minority in the Council of Ministers.

For most of 1989, therefore, there was a stand-off in the Council of Ministers on this issue. Although there was less resistance to the liberalization of value-added services, such as videotext, automatic financial transactions and electronic mail, there was considerable opposition (led by Belgium, with the support of France, Spain, Italy and Greece) to ending the PTT monopoly of basic data communication by public packet-switching.

The argument here, unlike that on the terminal-equipment directive, was therefore over substance as well as procedure, resulting in widespread opposition to the services directive at the Telecommunications Council meeting on 27 April 1989. Both Britain and Germany made it clear that they supported the objective of the services directive, but, although Germany joined ten other member-states in condemning the use of Article 90, the United Kingdom did not join them. UNICE was swift to express its 'deep dismay' on behalf of European business and industry that some member-states were putting pressure on the Commission to withdraw its draft directive, and a considerable lobbying effort by users and service providers was mounted.

The Commission decided in June 1989 to proceed notwithstanding with the services directive under Article 90(3), and when it formally promulgated the directive in June 1990 it could not exclude a later challenge in the ECJ from France, Spain and other member-states. It ruled out using Article 100a, since it knew that it would in any event encounter a substantial blocking minority, led by France, in the Council of Ministers. The Commission justifies its use of Article 90(3) for the services directive on the ground that this is not a legislative directive but a law-enforcement directive in a situation in which the competition policy of the EEC Treaty is being breached, and a series of ECJ enforcement actions against the member-states would be cumbersome and not provide the necessary guidance for the future.

Nevertheless, the absence in the Article 90 process of any formalized consultation with the Council of Ministers or the European Parliament, or even informal consultations to generate interest-group support for the measure, must be considered a serious flaw. The Commission sought to forestall opposition to the use of Article 90(3) (EEC) for the services directive by affirming that it would not issue the directive until the Council had passed the Open Network Provision (ONP), which lays down ground-rules for common technical standards, minimum-service provisions and harmonization of principles governing tariff structures.

Initially France attempted to limit entry of new competitors to basic packet-switching services – a position strongly opposed by both the British and the German governments and a coalition of EC user groups, who wanted only infrastructure, voice telephony and telex to be reserved to the PTOs, and wanted open access for all other areas. Eventually, at a Telecommunications Council meeting on 7 December 1989, a compromise was reached on opening data services to competition. The member-states agreed to liberalize all value-added network services from April 1990, and to end the PTO monopoly of basic data transmission by 1993, thus opening up the 75bn ecus market for telecommunications services. Member-states with poorly developed infrastructures (Spain, Portugal and Greece) will be able to ask the Commission for an extension of their monopolies until 1996.

The other part of the package, the revised text of the Commission's Article 90 directive on telecommunications services, explicitly leaves open the possibility that member-states may impose licence obligations for some services, allowing them to fulfil public-service obligations. All such licence conditions would, however, be vetted by the Commission before they could be imposed, so as to ensure that they conform to EC competition law, and are transparent and non-discriminatory. This compromise on the ONP framework directive and the services directive was finally agreed by the Telecommunications Council of Ministers in June 1990.[15]

The last of the Green Paper's major proposals for directives implementing a single market in telecommunications is the 'Directive on the procurement procedures by public contracting entities in telecommunications', one of the hitherto excluded sectors. This directive, on which the Council agreed a common position in February 1990 and which was approved in September 1990, breaks new ground in the public-procurement field by covering bodies operating on the basis of special or exclusive rights granted by member-states, irrespective of their legal status. This measure is intended to ensure competitive and non-discriminatory procurement, an objective that the British government strongly supports, although it had earlier hoped to exclude the private PTOs in Britain on the ground that they were already exposed to sufficient competition in the United Kingdom to ensure open procurement in telecommunications, and that therefore the privately owned network operators should not be subjected to the burden of demonstrating compliance (see Chapter 3).

Perhaps the most successful element of the Green Paper's proposals was the establishment in April 1988 of the European Telecommunications Standards Institute (ETSI), created by a decision of the PTT-Directors-General of the CEPT, the European PTT Conference. ETSI is charged with developing European standards for telecommunications equipment and services, and is independent of both CEPT (which by definition is dominated by the PTTs) and CEN/CENELEC. It has a membership of just over 130, drawn from governments, PTTs, private-service operators, manufacturers (including non-European firms with a base in Europe), users and the Commission. The open membership policy is explicitly intended to increase European influence in international standards-setting bodies, in the hope that international standards based on the European pattern will give European telecommunications firms greater export opportunities – although it will increase competition for these firms within Europe itself.

Under the PTT-dominated process, network operators had been able to work closely with their chosen producers, whose risks in R&D were reduced by the certainty of obtaining supply contracts. Involving manufacturers and users in the development process is therefore a necessary concomitant of open procurement. The involvement of users in ETSI (although some may in fact simply be suppliers in disguise) is another innovation, in keeping with a more market-oriented approach. ETSI clearly plays a vital role in the process of liberalization that is set in train by the Green Paper – in the terminal equipment field, ISDN and digital mobile communications, for example – and thus far has shown itself to be somewhat speedier and certainly more representative than CEPT had been. None the less, some observers have noted that a number of the working groups are chaired by CEPT personnel, and that, when comparing the British and the German influence on ETSI deliberations, the German advantage lay in its strong, well-funded and staffed industry group representation.[16]

Conclusion

Technology change has made telecommmunications no longer a natural monopoly, and globalization makes competition, rather than existing national regulatory regimes, the most potent force in determining the development of the sector. The prospect of transnational companies moving their communications centres to another EC country with a more advantageous telecommunications structure is a very real one, and has certainly been a major factor in the rapid liberalization of the German telecommunications sector (as, indeed, have the new imperatives of upgrading East Germany's communications infrastructure as part of the unification process).

Thus far the Community's initiatives in telecommunications have been clearly aimed at liberalization and have also had some deregulatory impact (although less than the influence of market forces and technological change). What has not yet been addressed is whether the regulatory function of the Community's institutions should extend beyond the enforcement of Community competition policy. It is not yet clear whether some EC-level institution similar to the Federal Communications Commission (FCC) in the United States, or Oftel in the United Kingdom, is required, insulated from the political pressures of the Council or the technocratic ambitions of the Commission. Developments in communications technology, notably the introduction of ISDN, are making the boundaries between the reserved sectors (network infrastructure, voice telephony and telex) and the rest of telecommunications/ telematics increasingly unsustainable. The problems of nationally based regulation are compounded by the movement of equipment manufacturers, such as Siemens, into network and service provision, and the expansion of PTOs, such as British Telecom and DBP Telekom, into other markets in the EC and beyond.

At company level, there are clear signs that both equipment manufacturers and PTOs are now penetrating each other's markets; the recent consortial activity for personal communication network licences in the United Kingdom, and for cellular mobile communication licences in Germany, is evidence of this. The strong position of Siemens in telecommunications equipment (there is no 'Community champion' headquartered in the United Kingdom) means that Germany will maintain its capabilities in this area, whatever rationalization takes place in the EC sector overall. This does not necessarily mean that Germany will welcome foreign incursions into its telecommunications equipment industry; it is notable that neither the Japanese nor the American Bell regional-operating companies have a significant presence in the German market, whereas all seven 'Baby Bells' are involved in the United Kingdom. In this connection, Britain may well decide – as it has done in the car industry – that it is better to invite foreigners to manufacture in the United Kingdom than to endure a deteriorating trade balance.

There is also reason to believe that PTOs are finding it more difficult to maintain a united front – on creating a data-network-service project that is pan-European and PTO-managed, for example – and that liberalization has sharpened differences between them. Broadly speaking, both the British and the German governments are on the same, pro-liberalization, side in Council debates, and DBP Telekom and BT both have sufficient involvement outside their home markets to have a vested interest in assuring liberalization in all but basic-network operation and telephony/telex.

Lastly, it now seems clear that the United Kingdom is no longer far in front of Germany where liberalization of telecommunications is concerned. In Germany, liberalization of areas in which DBP Telekom is not already entrenched (satellite communication and value-added services) has progressed further and faster than has been the case in Britain, which had a head start in the process of liberalization and privatization. What remains to be seen in the German case is whether it will be possible to maintain cross-subsidies and promote social objectives if liberalization and increased competition from other telecommunications technologies and service providers narrows the revenue base of DBP Telekom. It is at this point that the emerging debate on the social dimension of the Community's telecommunications policy will assume a critical importance, and the essential differences between the British and the German approaches to liberalization will become manifest.

6

FINANCIAL SERVICES

The significance of the sector
The financial sector as a whole is of special interest in that it epitomizes
the central issues of the 1992 process: whether, on balance, the single
market initiative involves deregulation or reregulation, and whether
structural and strategic change in the sector is policy- or market-led.
Financial services now contribute about 8% of the Community's GDP –
twice that of agriculture – and credit and insurance services account for
about 6% of all inputs into industry. To the extent that the creation of a
single financial market enables capital to be allocated more efficiently,
this would produce significant benefits to the EC's economy as a whole.

The financial services area is thus of critical importance in promoting
the economic development and integration of the EC. Both British and
German institutions are key players. The volume of business transacted
in London in insurance, shares and banking is much greater than in any
other EC country, while in Germany the development of universal banks
offering the whole range of financial services (*Allfinanz*) is the most advanced in the EC. The Cecchini Report pointed out that integration of
European markets in financial services would produce substantial economic gains in terms of an increase in competition, the provision of more
efficient services to business, and macroeconomic benefits arising from
risk-pooling and equalization of interest rates.[1] The 'costs of non-
Europe' study projected a possible gain of 22bn ecus in consumer surplus
in the eight markets studied (France, Germany, Italy, Spain, the United
Kingdom and Benelux) from integration of financial-service activity,
largely from erosion of price differentials between existing national

markets.[2] The study estimated that these would reduce the cost of banking services in Germany by 13% and in the United Kingdom by 9%, and lower the cost of stock exchange transactions by 6% in both countries. With regard to banking, the study concluded that 'the barriers to trade lie not so much in overt, discriminatory rules and regulations, but rather in national practices that apply equally to both domestic and foreign-controlled banks', such as differences in licensing, minimum capital and solvency requirements, and territorial restrictions.[3]

These barriers have the effect of limiting competitive pressures within national financial systems, quite apart from the high costs of market entry (the establishment of a network of branches is a necessity in retail banking) and the need to adapt to local customs in order to gain access to consumers. Despite the lack of progress in achieving harmonization at the Community level, some significant changes have occurred as a result of changes in global developments. In banking, for example, the wholesale/corporate sector has become more international and integrated as a result of increased competition. The retail/personal banking sector, however, remains confined to national systems because of the need for a branch network and because of the small size of individual transactions.

These strong impulses towards global integration of markets confront entrenched and extensive regimes of national supervision and regulation, resulting in debates about the desirability of international coordination of regulation through such bodies as the Bank for International Settlements (BIS). Thus the EC's attempts to create a single market for financial services have not only to win the support of the member-states, but also to be consistent with (or adaptable to) wider regimes, and flexible enough to meet changing conditions. In some respects, elements of the emerging EC regime may turn out to be prototypes for wider international agreements, with considerable advantages accruing to those financial firms that have already adapted successfully.

The international structure and evolution of the financial-services industry has been substantially influenced in recent years by four factors: deregulation in some major markets; a more competitive environment; new technology; and increasing internationalization of finance. The EC's 1992 initiative will represent a significant change in the market environment for all suppliers of financial services, since previous attempts to create a European common market in financial services had been based on attempts to harmonize regulation and supervisory arrangements, and, as a result of political and bureaucratic barriers, had made very slow progress. Because the sector as a whole is so closely connected to national monetary and payments systems, financial services have tended to be more regulated and protected at the national level than most other sectors.

The Commission's programme

Although it is by no means certain that a single market in financial services will emerge by the end of 1992, the dramatic progress over the past five years in enacting the White Paper's proposals must give grounds for optimism.

The most important stimulus to the liberalization of financial services was the Council of Ministers' decision in July 1988 to eliminate residual controls on cross-border capital movements by July 1990, with grace periods for some member-states (Spain and Ireland until 1992, Greece and Portugal until 1995). Neither Germany nor the United Kingdom have any exchange controls, so the liberalization of capital movements will have little direct effect on British and German financial institutions in their home markets, but it makes it much easier for them to expand operations elsewhere.

Although the Second Banking Coordination Directive (SBCD) is the centrepiece in the Commission's programme, it had been preceded in February 1987 by a directive liberalizing cross-border transactions in unit trusts, unlisted securities and long-term trade credits, which came into effect in October 1989.

In 1989, good progress was made on the four other directives applicable to credit institutions; the Council approved the directives on own funds (i.e. bank capital), solvency ratios and branch accounts, and the European Parliament's amendments to the consumer-credit directive were due for final Council consideration. In the field of investment services, the Council adopted in November 1989 the insider-trading directive, making insider-trading illegal for the first time in Germany, Italy, Belgium and Ireland.[4]

Other important measures dealing with transactions in securities – notably the investment-services directive and the directive on market risk – await further discussion. The Commission has indicated informally that, given the predominant position of banking in the financial-services sector, it does not want to delay progress in opening up the banking market. Its view is that there is time to finalize and implement the securities directives before the SBCD comes into effect in January 1993. Some observers consider this to be a very optimistic view, given that the investment-services directive is trying to achieve in one step what took a decade to implement in banking. The considerable progress in the passage of the various insurance directives, discussed in the second half of this chapter, does, however, give some support to the credibility of the Commission's timetable.

Certainly the globalization of financial markets and the momentum acquired by the single-market initiative have had a significant impact on providers of financial services. Although it is most unlikely that there will be an integrated EC market by the end of 1992, there has been a flurry of acquisitions, joint ventures and cross-border expansion by financial institutions from within and outside the Community. The reorganization and rationalization of the smaller local banks in Germany, the significant increase in foreign stake-building in British insurance companies, and the acquisition of insurance and investment firms by banks are all part of this process.

The Second Banking Coordination Directive

In February 1988, the Commission's draft for an SBCD introduced a significant new approach to achieving integration of national financial systems in the EC. In many respects, it may be seen as a prototype for the regulatory structure of financial services as a whole in the Community, and, as will be seen below, its definition of reciprocity is mirrored in other single market measures. The Commission's proposals to create a single market in financial services derived from three main objectives: first, to liberalize capital movements; second, to enable financial services to be sold across borders; and, third, to extend to all financial firms in the EC the right of establishment in other member-states. Instead of the earlier approach of requiring a high degree of prior harmonization, the SBCD sought to establish two new principles: first, that a credit institution should be regulated and supervised by its home-country government; and, second, that there should be mutual recognition by all member governments of each other's regulatory and supervisory arrangements.

The SBCD was adopted by the Council in December 1989, and, together with the solvency-ratio directive (which sets out capital requirements for banks, and is closely modelled on the 1988 Basle Agreement developed by the Cooke Committee for the BIS), will take effect in January 1993.[5]

The SBCD is based upon a 'single-licence' principle, with home-country control, so that a bank that has been authorized by its home supervisor to engage in activities specified in the directive (including, in addition to lending and deposit-taking, money transmission, securities-trading and provision of financial advice) may engage in them throughout the Community, without further authorization, even in countries in which credit institutions are barred from the activities concerned. The effect of this will be to give considerable advantage to countries, such as the United Kingdom and Germany, in which universal banking is permitted, and increase the pressure for liberalization in countries, such as Italy and Denmark, with more restrictive regulations.[6]

The most controversial aspect of the first draft of the SBCD was Article 9, governing reciprocal access for Community banks to third countries. The Commission revised the original text (which proposed the automatic triggering of a review process whenever a bank from outside the EC sought a licence) in the spring of 1989, following protests not only from member-states – notably the United Kingdom, Germany and the Netherlands – but also from the United States and Japan.

Under revised Article 9 of the SBCD, the Commission need report only periodically on the accessibility of third countries for Community banks; if EC banks do not enjoy 'national treatment' (that is, rights comparable with those of indigenous banks), the Community may take retaliatory measures, such as suspending or delaying requests for authorization – a measure similar to section 183 of the 1985 Financial Services Act in the United Kingdom. Article 9 goes on to empower the Commission to draw up proposals for the Council to go a stage further and negotiate 'comparable access', or the same rights for EC banks in a third country as those enjoyed by third-country banks in the EC, although it does not make entirely clear whether the Council or the Commission is ultimately responsible for implementation of reciprocity policy.[7] Overall, the compromise text of Article 9 seems to have satisfied most initial objectors and serves as the model for Community reciprocity provisions in other areas of financial services, such as insurance and investment.

Financial services in Britain and Germany
The interviews conducted for this study suggest that the EC's initiatives in financial services will not have as great an effect on the retail/personal sector as the Cecchini Report envisaged. Local-market presence and consumer acceptance are vital in both retail banking and mass-risk insurance; penetrating foreign markets, even with a substantial local presence, is a long and difficult process. It is unlikely, therefore, that the

single market in financial services will be rapidly achieved simply because the Commission's package of legislation is implemented. If uni-
versality of regulation and similarity of legal requirements were enough
to ensure penetration of foreign banking markets, one might have expected the Scottish banks – which have long enjoyed such an integrated
regime vis-à-vis England – to have penetrated more extensively the
market south of the border.

None the less, our findings do tend to confirm the conclusion of
Xavier Vives that the main effect of integration will be to increase
competition or to reduce collusion and regulatory capture within national
markets, but not to remove all economic barriers to entry.[8] This inten-
sification of competition will stimulate linkages between financial
institutions – through acquisitions, mergers and cross-shareholdings – to
mitigate the effects of increased competition.

Both Britain and Germany have strong indigenous financial services
sectors, and have the most liberal policies towards them of any EC
member-states. In the United Kingdom, the financial sector has long
been fully exposed to foreign competition, has a history of light and
flexible regulation (at least until the advent of the Financial Services
Act), and, since 1979, freedom from exchange controls. There has been a
widely held view, reinforced in DTI and CBI promotional literature on
the single market, that the United Kingdom has much to gain from the
liberalization of financial services markets within Europe, 'given the
highly developed state and openness of our markets in relation to many
of the European centres'.[9] Certainly the Cecchini Report concurred with
this optimistic view, citing Britain as the greatest potential beneficiary
from integrated financial markets in Europe, although it should be
pointed out that Cecchini was calculating potential gains to consumers,
and much of these savings would come from reduced profits in the very
lucrative consumer-credit operations of financial institutions in the
United Kingdom.

In the summer of 1989, the Bank of England published a comprehensive and illuminating survey of the attitude of the UK financial-services
industry towards the single European market.[10] The survey indicated a
widespread belief among market practitioners that completion of the
internal market would offer more opportunities than threats in the long
run, but that the main developments in the market would derive as much
from the psychological impact of the 1992 process, prompting firms to
review and revise their strategies, as from the direct effect of new EC
legislation in liberalizing financial services.

The survey found that the single-market initiative would have little impact on wholesale financial products and services, for which, for the most part, a unified market already exists, but, at the same time, the retail-banking level – while offering much scope for change and expansion as hitherto restricted markets are liberalized – would develop only slowly as consumer attitudes changed. The retail level also presented more obstacles in distribution, since acquisition of a retail network would be very expensive, and restrictions would remain on local conduct of business – advertising, fund composition, and so on.[11] The Bank of England's survey concluded that 'while markets were expected to draw closer together, as a result of competitive pressures, the development of anything like a true EC single market for most kinds of financial service would take many years. National markets were expected to remain largely distinct for some considerable time to come.'[12]

In general, the firms surveyed by the Bank believed that their basic strategy towards the Community would not be changed by the creation of the single market; smaller firms with limited international business stressed that securing their UK homebase would remain their prime objective. The largest banks surveyed certainly aimed to compete on a Community-wide basis, but were not intending to seek cross-border mergers with, or acquisitions of, other large banks or financial institutions – purchases of smaller competitors or niche players were thought more likely. Indeed, the survey clearly indicated that large cross-border mergers were very difficult to implement effectively, with differences of financial, managerial and corporate culture presenting even more formidable problems than they do in mergers involving commercial or industrial firms.

Where mergers and acquisitions do occur, the respondents in the survey expected them to be between institutions involved in different, but complementary, businesses (banking and insurance, for example), or between second-tier institutions compelled to follow defensive strategies – often with both firms coming from the same country, as has recently been the case in Spanish banking. Spain, France and Italy emerged from the survey as the most attractive markets, largely because the new opportunities would be greatest, while Germany was seen as less promising a market, because of the closeness of banking relationships and the conservatism of consumers. Opportunites do exist, though, notably in the pensions and life-insurance sectors.[13]

Although a comparable survey is not available for Germany, all the available evidence indicates a similar level of optimism and confidence regarding the opportunities of the single market in financial services. Deutsche Bank is the most prominent example of a financial institution committed to a strategy of pan-European, universal banking, and for some years it has sought to build up a commercial-banking network through acquisitions, such as its purchase in 1986 of Banca d'America e d'Italia (from Bank of America), which gained it 100 branches for $603m. (It has recently moved to acquire full ownership of Spain's Banco Comercial Transatlantico.)[14] In August 1989, Deutsche Bank announced that it was bringing ahead to September its long-awaited move into the life-insurance business by establishing a fully owned subsidiary, Lebensversicherungs-AG der Deutschen Bank, in Wiesbaden.[15] Commerzbank has chosen a different strategy, preferring to set up operating agreements with Banco di Roma, Crédit Lyonnais and Banco Hispano Americano. Some observers have seen this strategy as less expensive but ultimately less rewarding. Yet another strategy is exemplified by the exclusive marketing agreement announced in March 1989 between Dresdner Bank and Allianz, Europe's biggest insurance company, based on Allianz's previous agreement with Bayerische Hypobank.[16]

As in the United Kingdom, the profitability of retail-banking operations tends to undercut suggestions that Germany is overbanked, and the high cost of entry into retail financial services will deter most outsiders. In wholesale banking, however, notably in mergers and acquisitions (expected to be of growing importance in the run-up to 1992), foreign competition is intensifying. The indigenous banks have an advantage in their long-standing relationships with, and holdings in, many of the most important German companies. (Deutsche Bank owns 28% of Daimler Benz, and, although the SBCD limits single bank holdings in outside companies to 60% of shareholders' funds, with no more than 15% in any one firm, the shares are carried at book value, and for Deutsche Bank amount to less than 40% of its current share price.)[17]

Although it is relatively simple to obtain official authorization for foreign financial institutions to set up in Germany – so that the SBCD's single licence will have little effect – German financial markets are subject to exceptionally strict regulation, extending to vetting financial products and specifying what may be sold, so that life-insurance policies vary little in content (see the section on insurance, below). The prospect of home-country regulation under the SBCD has prompted the larger German banks to press for policies to expand and strengthen national-securities markets, which have long been fragmented and underdeveloped, particularly with regard to the range of authorized market instruments and the number of equities institutional investors may hold in their portfolios.[18]

The German decision to impose a 10% witholding tax – rescinded in 1989 after much protest – was seen in Frankfurt as an example of Bonn's lack of vision or strategy in dealing with international financial competition. It remains to be seen whether the current enthusiasm among the German universal banks for *Allfinanz* – the provision of all financial services under one roof – will be replicated elsewhere in the Community in the approach to 1992. The relative lack of success of financial institutions in London after the 'big bang', when they moved into the securities business, would seem to indicate that universal banking is not a panacea.

Creating a single market in insurance

Differences between the German and the British insurance sectors are marked, in terms of both regulation and market structures. The British insurance sector appears to be an entirely free, competitive market, which could only benefit from the single-market initiative, whereas the German insurance market is highly regulated and less competitive. Thus, whereas the British insurance industry seems to push for the liberalization of the EC insurance market, the German insurance industry gives the impression of being far less enthusiastic about liberalization and of viewing EC initiatives in this field with scepticism. Consumer protection through heavy regulation of both companies and policies has become part of the German 'architecture of the state' and can be counted among the sacred cows that have to be slaughtered with the advent of the single market.

In a recent survey, managers of insurance companies were asked to assess the regulatory intensity of the different EC insurance markets.[19] The Netherlands and the United Kingdom were regarded as having the lowest degree of regulatory intervention, and Germany the highest.

In Germany, the advent of the single market has given increased impetus to proposals for liberalization of its insurance industry. In 1987, a committee of experts (the Deregulierungskommission), set up by the Federal government, was given the task of assessing the scope for deregulation in a number of sectors. Its interim report, published in April 1990, advocates extensive deregulation of the insurance sector, as did an earlier report published by the German monopolies commission in 1988.[20]

The insurance market in the EC has considerable growth potential: in 1986, premium income per capita was as high as $1,747 in Switzerland

and $1,536 in the United States, but only $465 for the EC as a whole; within the Community, premium income per capita ranged from 994 ecus for the FRG, 820 ecus for the United Kingdom, and only 140 ecus for Spain. With increasing wealth, particularly in the south European countries, and demographic changes, which are leading to greater mistrust of state pension schemes, spending on insurance in the EC is likely to continue to increase.

In 1988, the 'cost of non-Europe' study found that life insurance in Britain was 30% cheaper, and commercial fire and theft insurance in Italy was 245% more expensive, than the average of the four cheapest national prices within the EC. Although the methods of calculation can be criticized, and the nature of the risks involved may differ (e.g. different climatic conditions, different mortality rates), these figures nevertheless provide some useful indication of the potential price adjustments and the potential advantages for the British insurance sector in an open market.

German insurance companies remain strong on their national market, but they have less of a presence in other markets than do British firms. The latter have 608 establishments in 43 countries world-wide; German insurers have only 120 in 17 countries. There are 42 British establishments in Germany, but only 10 German firms in the United Kingdom. Within the EC itself, British companies also have a greater presence, with 299 establishments, compared with 101 for German and 85 for French companies.[21]

The British also seem to be in a stronger position when market share is measured by premium revenue. The British industry earns 35% of its premium revenue abroad (Lloyds excluded), whereas German firms manage a mere 3.7%. This disparity, however, is largely due to the fragmented nature of the German insurance industry and the essentially domestic orientation of the small- and medium-size firms; Allianz, by far the largest German insurer, earns 40% of its premium revenue abroad. The national market shares of gross premium income in the Community also show the British as ahead in life insurance (27.5bn ecus as against 23.6bn ecus for Germany), but behind in non-life, with 24.9bn ecus against 32.1bn for German firms.

Liberalization of the EC insurance market
Progress on cross-border provision of services, which could bring about a genuine EC-wide insurance market, has been extremely slow. After the adoption in 1964 of the reinsurance directive and the subsequent break-

through in the passage of the first directive on non-life insurance in 1973 and the first life-insurance directive in 1979 – which harmonized fundamental conditions for authorization of insurance companies as well as rules about their solvency – it became relatively straightforward for a company whose head office was situated in one member-state to open a branch in another member-state. However, any branch so established still has to comply with the regulations of the national market in which it operates. This right of establishment gives insurers access to twelve national markets, rather than creating a single European market.

The initial proposal submitted by the Commission in 1975 for a second non-life insurance directive covering services made no progress for twelve years. It was only when the Commission tried to extend the *Cassis de Dijon* approach to the insurance sector and started Article 169 procedures (for EEC Treaty infringement) against France, Germany, Denmark and Italy that the proposed insurance-services directive came back into the limelight.

The most significant case against a member country was the so-called *Schleicher* case against Germany, instigated by a German insurance broker who had been fined by the German insurance regulatory agency, BAV (Bundesaufsichtsamt für das Versicherungswesen), for finding commercial insurance for his German clients in London.[22] Seven member-states joined this action: two on the side of the Commission, which supported Schleicher (the Netherlands and the United Kingdom), and the other five (Belgium, France, Denmark, Ireland and Italy) on the side of the FRG. In December 1986, the ECJ ruled in favour of the Commission, finding that the 1983 amendment of German insurance law (VAG), implementing the EC first-life and co-insurance directives, infringed Germany's obligations under Articles 59 and 60 (EEC) – freedom to provide services – by requiring that provider firms are established in Germany. However, the Court upheld other – non-discriminatory – requirements of the German insurance law. In practice, this meant that a national supervisory authority could still impose very tight rules, as long as it did not explicitly require establishment.

It is not widely known that, since 1901, German law has allowed consumers to obtain a policy directly from a foreign insurer by correspondence. It is considered that, by purchasing such *assurance sauvage*, policy-holders deliberately place themselves out of the reach of their national supervisory authority. Hence, a concept akin to the 'own-initiative' suggested in the Commission proposal for the life-services directive, is not unfamiliar to German law, nor, of course, to British and Dutch legislation. In other EC countries, it was still considered an offence for a resident consumer to purchase insurance cover from an insurer abroad. The practical economic impact of allowing the purchase of insurance by correspondence is, however, insignificant. It is estimated that less than 1% of German life-insurance policies are obtained in this way.

In its ruling on the *Schleicher* case, the ECJ explicitly mentioned the proposal for the non-life services directive, making the distinction between large (commercial) risks and mass (individual-consumer) risks. It argued that commercial risks do not require the same level of protection for the policy-holder as mass risks, and would not necessarily have to comply with tight regulations in the country of destination. It did not, however, specify any criteria for the distinction between commercial and non-commercial risks.

After agreements on liberalization of capital movements and the passage of the SBCD in 1989, the focus of attention within the Commission's DG XV (the directorate-general dealing with financial services) has now shifted to insurance. The 1985 White Paper, the *Schleicher* case and the introduction of Article 100a majority voting in the Single European Act (SEA) have therefore produced a certain impetus, which is helping to end the stalemate on insurance. The importance of the SEA is shown by the fact that the second non-life insurance directive was adopted by the Council in June 1988 in spite of Greece and Portugal voting against it.[23] The life-services directive was finally adopted in October 1990. Despite its opposition to the 'broker clause' (see below), Germany had already voted in favour of a common position in December 1989 at the meeting of the Internal Market Council. The merger-control regulation, which was very important from an *Ordnungspolitik* point of view, was adopted at the same meeting.

Sir Leon Brittan, the Commissioner responsible (for the first time since the establishment of the Commission) for both competition policy and financial services, has made it clear that he wants to push through the Council those directives that are still needed to liberalize the insurance market. In November 1989, Brittan announced that the liberalization of the insurance sector will be achieved not by detailed legislation, but by the adoption of two 'framework directives' – one for life and one for non-life. These directives will apply the 'single-passport' system already adopted in the banking sector – a move which the United Kingdom has long advocated. The Commission submitted the proposal for the non-life framework directive in July 1990 and intends to complete legislation of the life framework directive by the end of 1981.

Regulation of the insurance sector in Germany and the United Kingdom

Domestic and foreign insurance companies doing business in Germany are supervised by the BAV (itself supervised by the Ministry of Finance), which is considered – at least in Germany – to be the world's toughest insurance supervisory authority. Through two laws, the VAG supervisory and licensing law (Versicherungsaufsichtsgesetz), and the VVG insurance contract law (Gesetz über den Versicherungsvertrag), the protection of policyholders, third parties and beneficiaries was promoted by a significant degree of state supervision of insurance-company structure, permissible forms of insurance contract, and valuation of assets and liabilities. The principle of specialization (Spartentrennung) until recently prevented composite (life and general) insurance companies from doing business in Germany, since the BAV would authorize only those insurance providers that offered the various categories of insurance through legally separate companies. As a result of EC legislation, and despite German opposition, this specialization requirement has now been abolished for liability and credit insurance, and also for life insurance services (although only provisionally in the case of life insurance that it provided on the active initiative of the insurance company, the position on which will be reviewed in 1995).

In 1989/90, debate on amendment of the VAG centred on whether it should be limited to the implementation of the EC directives, or whether it should be used as an opportunity to introduce more far-reaching national deregulatory measures and to anticipate the internal market by immediately adopting the lower threshold of the second non-life directive – a move favoured by the VAG, but not by the insurers. The GDV, the Association of German Insurers, argued that its members would be exposed to full competition on their own market, but could compete only for the 'very large risks' on other EC markets – a situation that British insurers had faced for some years.

Eventually it was a compromise position that was approved by the Bundestag in June 1990, more or less confining amendment of the VAG to the implementation of the EC directives. In this way, the German government hoped to avoid a repetition of the chaos caused in 1989, when it had been forced to withdraw its investment – witholding tax in response to pressure from German investors and the financial community.

The VVG, the insurance contract law, applies to most types of insurance, with the notable exception of reinsurance and marine insurance. It restricts the freedom of choice of the legal form of the contract by stipulating the conditions of validity of the insurance contract, its composition, its duration and how it can be transmitted. The VVG also contains stipulations about the duties of insurers and policyholders, cancellation rights and rights of third parties against the insurer. In contrast to British practice, it represents considerable interference on the part of the state in what is in essence a private contract, and is a significant barrier to product innovation and differentiation.

Both domestic and foreign companies must have general policy conditions and documents approved. However, under the second non-life directive, it is no longer possible for the BAV to require approval (or systematic notification) of general and special policy conditions and premium scales for large commercial risks. Occasional provision of such information may be required for the purpose of verifying compliance with laws, regulations and administrative provisions, but this requirement may not constitute a prior condition for an insurance company to be able to carry out its activities.

In comparison with Germany and most other countries, the United Kingdom has a very liberal regulatory system. The Secretary of State for Trade and Industry is the supervisory authority for all classes of insurance, providing authorization for firms to underwrite one or more of the seven classes of long-term and the eighteen classes of general non-life insurance policies. Foreign insurers and investors are permitted to enter the UK domestic market for direct insurance, or to set up a reinsurance base in London, but (as with British firms) they must obtain an authorization from the Secretary of State for Trade and Industry.

The Insurance Companies Act (ICA) of 1982 is the primary law regulating the British insurance industry. British insurers do not face any stringent restrictions on the form of policy contracts, levels of premium rates or disposition of investment funds. Thus, British life insurers invest over half of their fixed assets in shares, whereas German life insurers may not exceed 20% (and in fact have only 4% of their assets currently invested in shares).

Protection against the insolvency of an insurance company is provided for in the ICA, although application of the ICA to Lloyd's is limited to the annual solvency certificate for the society as a whole, rather than for individual underwriting members, their syndicates and managing agency companies. Lloyd's therefore remains basically a self-regulating insurance market.

While it was possible for Lloyd's to retain its particular legal identity within the United Kingdom, its operations in other EC member-states were more difficult, since it is not a company. Instead of establishing branches elsewhere in the Community, which would have involved high compliance costs, Lloyd's adjusted its operations to provide reinsurance in foreign markets. Lloyd's has, more than any other British insurer, eagerly awaited the adoption of the services directives, through which it hopes to gain improved access to the EC market and make significant gains in the German market and elsewhere.

The initial draft of the second life directive excluded much of the composite insurance business from the freedom to provide services – a significant problem for Lloyd's and other composite insurers, which sell approximately 45% of life policies in the EC. In its March 1990 proposal, which was the basis for the final life-services directive, the Commission has extended the freedom to provide insurance services to composite companies, although this extension is only on a provisional basis and will have to be reviewed before the end of 1995. This suits the British insurance industry, but was opposed by both the German insurance sector and the Bundestag.[24]

The Financial Services Act (FSA) of 1985 changes the regulatory system under the 1982 ICA. As far as their marketing activities are concerned, the insurers have either to join one of the self-regulating organizations (SROs) or to become directly regulated for those activities by the Securities and Investment Board (SIB). Responsibility for prudential and financial supervision of insurance firms still lies, however, with the DTI.

The FSA also amends the rules set out in the 1977 Insurance Brokers (Registration) Act. All brokers are registered with the Insurance Broker's Registration Council, which is a Recognized Professional Body (RPB) and which is responsible for day-to-day regulation established by the FSA. The Broker's Registration Council lays down and monitors minimum financial standards and codes of practice for registered brokers. As yet, the control over the distribution of insurance is less strict in Germany (because of the German government's unwillingness to infringe professional freedom, there are no restrictions on persons setting themselves up as brokers). Germany may have to introduce quality requirements after the expiry of the three-year transitional period.

Diverging positions on the life-services directive

The life-services directive was adopted after very intense discussions, which clearly brought out the divergent interests of British and German insurers as well as the contrasting national supervisory approaches. The potential economic impact of the directive is great, particularly in Germany, in which more than half of the 2.12m people in the EC's high-incomes category (over 200,000 DM per year) live. British insurers hope to be able to attract a big share of this market.

The main problem with the life-services directive, at least from the German perspective, was the 'own-initiative' concept and the role of brokers (Article 13). Whereas British insurers welcome the possibility for consumers to consult a broker, German insurers opposed the 'broker clause', both on the grounds of consumer protection and because they consider the clause to be inconsistent with the ECJ's 'insurance ruling', which they interpret as support for more harmonization before the opening-up of the market for mass risks. They further argue that allowing all EC citizens to purchase insurance via correspondence is already a big step forward, and the directive should have stopped there. Moreover, the directive leaves the concept of 'own initiative' vague, thereby opening the way for brokers to circumvent it. In other words, brokers will not, in practice, wait for customers to consult them, but will actively seek business. Once they have it, they will get the customer to sign a paper stating that they, the customers, approached the broker. Despite these reservations, the directive was adopted in October 1990.

The future of the insurance sector

There seems to be a general expectation that 1992 is going to lead to increased competition in the insurance sector, and that perhaps only a handful of companies will be able to establish themselves as pan-European players in the single market. In Germany, Allianz has been pursuing a pan-European acquisition strategy since the mid-1980s – even before the single-market programme. It has 14% of the life and 16% of the non-life insurance market in Germany, is number two in Austria and Italy (with a 10% market share, mainly as a result of a majority stake in RAS) and number seven in Spain (a 51% stake in Ercos was bought this year). In France, Allianz is now among the first ten insurers with a 3% market share after buying, in October 1989, a 50% stake in the insurance side of Compagnie de Navigation Mixte. In the United Kingdom, Allianz's market share is, however, only 1%. It acquired the Cornhill Group in 1986, after an unsuccessful bid for Eagle Star. As with other German companies, it has shifted its interest away from the EC market and towards Central and Eastern Europe in general and East Germany in particular. Allianz took a significant stake in the Deutsche Versicher-ungs-AG, the GDR insurance monopoly.[25]

As for the rest of the German industry, one must expect greater rationalization and consolidation. The small- and medium-sized companies are going to have to specialize if they wish to survive, and more mergers and acquisitions are to be expected. British insurers have probably realized more quickly than their German counterparts that tighter regulations for insurance than for banking may now lead to a competitive disadvantage for the insurance sector in the provision of financial services. For example, a single authorization will be all that is needed in order to provide investment services throughout the whole of the EC market; in the insurance sector, however, until the framework directives are adopted, positive action by national supervisory bodies will still be required before access in life insurance can be achieved.

The European Association of Insurers, the CEA, is aware of this and has pressed for the life-services directive to be seen in the context of the increased competition in the financial-services sector as a whole. Insurers have argued – and this is particularly a British concern – that all too often the draft for the second life directive has simply taken over wording from the second non-life directive, without taking into account the link between life and investment services in general.

Although German insurers expect some inroads into their markets through such broker-led business, especially from the United Kingdom, the larger firms doubt that there is much scope for increased market penetration. It is argued that British premiums are lower because of differences between British and German risk, or because British companies have been allowed to invest more in the bullish stock markets of the 1980s, such that the competitive advantage of the British will not be significant in the case of higher German risks and declining stock-markets. Indeed, some would argue that the only competitive advantage to be gained is in economies of scale in administration and marketing.

Another key factor in competitiveness is the renewed move in Germany towards *Allfinanz* (echoed, but to a lesser extent, in the United Kingdom and elsewhere), bringing insurance and banking closer together. The most striking example is that of Deutsche Bank in creating its own life assurance arm, Deutsche Lebensversicherung, which started business in September 1989.

But *Allfinanz* is not the only way to respond to the new European and global challenges. Most insurers are convinced that the old principle that 'all business is local' will prevail, even after the entry into force of the

EC directives. If this turns out to be true, much of the potential benefit from the freedom to provide cross-border services will be lost, since insurers will still need to have local market presence and a familiarity with local conditions.

The internal market will, however, certainly open up interesting opportunities in the non-life sector. It is estimated that, by 1993, 70% of the premium volume in commercial fire risks will fall under the heading 'large risks' and will thus be covered by the freedom to provide services granted by the non-life services directive.[26] Since July 1990, it has been possible to service a large share of the industrial, e.g. fire insurance, market, without being either established or authorized by the national supervisory authorities. Companies will be required to provide certification only in a few areas – e.g. solvency margins – in line with the requirements of the first non-life directive on establishment.

One of the surprising consequences of the directive may be that it could have a greater impact on insurance business carried out within a company's domestic market than it does on cross-border activities. Even smaller, domestically oriented, insurance firms will now be entirely free to formulate their own insurance contracts – a freedom that is taken for granted in Britain, but does not yet exist in Germany.

Another interesting new opportunity will be, for example, the creation of 'euro-policies' or of policies of a 'master-cover' type, which will allow an industrial company operating in several EC countries to insure against all risks with one insurer, who will then equalize the differences in conditions and cover. Even here, however, the impact of the directive is likely to be more indirect than direct. In order to keep their clients and to anticipate expected competition from abroad, domestic insurers will offer more policy-holder-friendly conditions, extended cover and/or lower premiums. In this way, consumers will benefit, but market penetration by foreign service providers will be limited, especially in Germany, in which insurance firms will now have much greater freedom to emulate insurance products offered by foreign competitors.

A further factor influencing the respective national approaches to regulation, and the competitive positions of the British and German industries, could be the existence of informal arrangements and self-regulation in the United Kingdom. As suggested above, our interviews have shown that many Germans believe that the British have established something of a functional equivalent to Germany's tight state supervision of companies and policy contents in the form of clubs of underwriters, 'breakfast arrangements' and self-regulated control of distribution. Some have suggested that, as the German market is deregulated, German companies will become exposed to increased competition. In Britain, however, such informal arrangements might continue to satisfy the British insurance sector's objectives of guaranteeing market stability without impeding competition. This could result in a competitive disadvantage for the German companies, which would face a greater need to adjust – especially as far as the control of distribution is concerned – once the restrictive authorization procedure for policy conditions has disappeared. Of course, the German industry may well be able to develop informal arrangements of its own. Indeed, the fact that the German regulatory regime is as it is can be traced to the effectiveness of the German trade associations in getting governments to translate their interests into legislation at the turn of the century. If the regulations are removed, informal arrangements may develop.

In considering informal arrangements, one must not neglect the role of the EC in competition policy. Since a ruling by the ECJ in 1987 against the Association of German Insurers, which had attempted to argue that Articles 85 and 86 (EEC) did not apply to insurance, it has been clear that the competition articles of the EEC Treaty also apply to the insurance sector. Given the difficulties for any one company in obtaining sufficient data in order to calculate risk correctly, there will always be a need for cooperation between companies in setting net premiums. Indeed, the Commission is currently discussing the possibility of a group exemption from Articles 85 and 86 (EEC), and has forwarded a proposal for an EC regulation.[27]

The creation of the internal market in insurance is also held up by unsolved questions, such as those about fiscal harmonization, which can be decided upon by the Council of Ministers only with unanimity. Indeed, national tax measures are sometimes seen as the most important impediment to the creation of a genuine single European market in insurance. British insurers feel they are at a disadvantage because there is no tax deduction for special reserves set up in order to smooth out the incidence of natural catastrophe losses.

Ultimately, the success of the single-market initiative in the insurance sector will depend on how strictly the rules are enforced and on how effectively the national supervisory authorities can cooperate (they already meet on a regular basis). The Commission, with only seven 'A' grade officials to cover insurance, is simply not able to monitor and regulate the whole EC. In EC regulation, as in national regulation, the key question is what balance will be struck between guaranteeing the protection of policy-holders and permitting product innovation. The approach followed by the Commission is clearly deregulatory, with far greater impact on Germany than on the already more liberal regime in Britain.

Small earthquake in financial services: not many dead

For the moment, the fears of British and German financial institutions that the single market for financial services would have protectionist overtones seem to have been allayed by the Council's agreement on the revised second banking directive's reciprocity provisions. Although much detailed work remains to be done, particularly on investment services, the liberalization of capital movements and the passage of the second banking directive have made it virtually certain that the planned single financial market will materialize, although it may be behind schedule (and, because of the concessions given to some member-states permitting them to maintain capital controls into the 1990s, the market will not in any case be Community-wide until 1995). For the most part, the changes have been supported by financial institutions in most member-states; and there has been no evidence of the sort of rearguard action that has characterized, for example, some of the debate on foreign competition in the automobile industry.

To some extent this may be due to a widespread acceptance by the firms involved that they will have no choice but to adapt as their customers adjust to the reality of the single market, and that in many cases their best chance of survival against domestic competition may be with a foreign partner. The Commission thus has allies, although they can be quite vociferous in their opposition if they perceive EC initiatives as involving over-regulation or the introduction of two-tier regulation with its attendant uncertainties. In some cases, the financial firms see the advent of home-country regulation of their foreign competitors as a lever to induce further liberalization and/or deregulation by their own government and regulatory authorities. This is certainly true of some British firms, which hope that the more onerous compliance aspects of the FSA will be eased as a result of foreign competition or the prospect of firms moving from London to a less rigorous regulatory climate. In other cases, such as the insurance sector in Germany, there has been a marked reluctance on the part of the firms themselves to go any faster than they are obliged by EC legislation.

It is clear that substantial progress has been made in the liberalization of banking – in both legislation and the alteration of corporate strategy to take the single market into account – and that very rapid progress has been made in insurance. Investment services, however, lag behind, and for this sector 1993 looks to be an increasingly unrealistic deadline. Given the trend in Germany toward *Allfinanz*, and the links between UK investment and insurance firms and continental banks, the asymmetry in creating a legislative and regulatory framework is unfortunate.

Making a reality of the single market in financial services will require convergence in national regulatory regimes and/or the creation of a European-level regulator. Industry experts are unanimous in considering a regulatory role to be inappropriate for the Commission's DG XV. Even if the requirements are fulfilled, and freedom of establishment enshrined, differences in conduct of business rules (and differences in consumer preferences) may inhibit the cross-border selling of financial products, whether direct or through local partners/intermediaries. For retail financial services, if not for the corporate market, a strong and committed local presence will be necessary, and few firms have the resources and distant time-horizons to engage in such cross-border activity. As with public procurement (see Chapter 3), the main effect of the single market will be to curb the most anti-competitive practices of domestic firms, and to prevent foreign predators from entering the market. American and Japanese firms might well behave less conservatively than their European competitors, thus precipitating more radical strategies by EC financial institutions.

7

BRITAIN AND GERMANY COMPARED

Our case-studies reveal interesting different national approaches on each issue. In part these stem from the particular sectoral features or the historical characteristics of previous regulatory policy or practice. However, they also reflect differences of a more fundamental kind between the overall policy approaches of each country to 1992. This concluding chapter explores these differences, examines how far each national approach is influenced by 1992 and considers the question of whether competition among rules is promoting any convergence.

The British approach

Britain in the 1980s was characterized by national policies of deregulation in which the role of the state in the economy was significantly decreased. A large programme of privatization reduced the size of the public sector and thus removed an important instrument of national industrial policy. At the beginning of the 1980s, Britain had a larger public sector than the Federal Republic, but by the end of the decade this situation had been reversed, even before German unification. In those areas in which public ownership in Britain did remain, a policy predicated on avoiding intervention ruled out the use of public ownership as a vehicle for promoting social or industrial policy objectives. This approach contrasts with the limited impact of privatization in the rest of the Community, including in the FRG. Public ownership in these other countries continues to offer a means of pursuing strategic national industrial interests, even though there have been few cases in which national governments have had such explicit policies.

Other instruments of national industrial policy have also been curtailed in Britain. Spending on national industrial subsidies has been significantly scaled back, with the result that British industry is less subsidized than German industry.[1] Somewhat belatedly, the British government has given strong support for more rigorous controls by the European Commission of national subsidies throughout the Community. It has also pursued a liberal approach on investment, in part because of the high level of outward investment from Britain, which is second only to American foreign direct investment, and in part as a means of attracting inward investment to revitalize the weak manufacturing base and to limit trade deficits.

Not only is inward investment encouraged, but there is no prejudice against foreign buyers acquiring key British companies – a process that is apparently not regarded as going against the national public interest. This view prevails despite the fact that, as Chapter 2 has shown, British companies face barriers to takeover in the rest of the Community. In contrast with Britain's resolute defence of formal political sovereignty, there has been no parallel defence of national industrial ownership. With certain limited exceptions, the Conservative governments of the 1980s have not seen it as their role to determine who owns and controls British business. Consequently, there has been no promotion of national champions, and even less desire to see the evolution of anything approaching the promotion of European champions or the defence of some kind of European industrial identity. Having rolled back the frontiers of the state in Britain, Mrs Margaret Thatcher's government was not about to accept an increase in intervention at an EC level.

It was therefore logical for the British government to stress the need for the single market to be open, especially in the period leading up to the Rhodes summit of December 1988, when the debate on fortress Europe was at its peak. Seen through British eyes, the liberalizing logic of the single market did not stop at the borders of the Community. In other words, the overall level of regulation in the British economy had already been – or was in the process of being – reduced as the 1992 programme was introduced. At the micro level of the 1992 directives, the programme therefore caused few problems for Britain. Indeed, the government actively favoured extending the liberalization already introduced at home to the EC and beyond, and in many cases Britain has been on the extreme liberal wing of the EC, pressing for more deregulation. This is clearly the case in telecommunications and financial services, but also in technical standards, in which the British were instrumental in pushing the deregulatory 'new approach'.

British policy was also directed towards reducing red tape at EC level – an aim that flowed directly from policies developed at a national level. In Britain a deregulation unit was established, first in the Department of Employment and later transferred, with Lord Young, to the DTI. The unit had the task of removing excessive or unnecessary regulatory requirements. In 1985, the British government successfully pressed for a similar unit to be established in the Commission, and for the introduction of procedures designed to help ensure that Brussels did not generate unnecessary red tape.

It would, however, be incorrect to characterize the British approach as wholesale deregulation. It has been clearly recognized that new regulation is sometimes needed to ensure liberalization in those markets in which competition is obstructed by non-statutory barriers, or to ensure that markets remain open. Within Britain, for example, behaviour in financial services markets is regulated by the new Financial Services Act of 1988, which accompanied the 'big bang' liberalization of the City of London. The British recognized the need for similar regulation at EC level. They therefore backed the directives on public procurement, despite the fact that these covered all purchasing entities – including the recently privatized British utilities – because such regulation was needed if a genuine opening of the EC markets was to be achieved. The field of takeovers is another clear case in which the British are the leading proponents of EC-level rules aimed at reducing or removing barriers to takeover elsewhere in the Community.

The British government also favours new regulation at an EC level in order to achieve more competition, hence its ultimate support of the EC regulation on merger control. Nevertheless, some ambiguity remains in the British approach to European competition policy. In several instances, specific national policy objectives have overridden the general desire to see an open and competitive market within Europe. In the case of the British Airways merger with British Caledonian, the British government jibbed at Commission intervention. The insistence on privatization also led the British government into conflict with the European Commission. The Rover case, in which the government concealed from the Commission (and indeed from the British Parliament) the scale of exchequer support for British Aerospace, the purchaser, was the most notorious, but by no means the only, case.

Yet there are clear limits to how far the British government is prepared to go in accepting European regulation. Whenever this increases the EC's discretionary powers – especially those of the European Commission – the British government, along with other governments, has obstructed any such shift in competence. For example, the British maintained a reservation on the merger-control regulation until they were confident that the Commission would not be given discretionary powers to approve mergers on grounds of international competition or industrial policy. In the field of public procurement, the British government blocked the Commission acquiring new powers to intervene in contract-award procedures.

The telecommunications sector is particularly illuminating as regards how much European regulation the British government is prepared to accept. When the European Commission used Article 90 (EEC) as a basis for directives aimed at opening the markets in telecommunications equipment and services, the British government was faced with a dilemma. Should it support the move because it would accelerate liberalization? Or should it oppose the use of Article 90 (EEC) because it would be an important precedent and would enlarge the scope for the use of discretionary powers by the Commission? In the end, the British decided not to challenge the Commission's move before the ECJ, but in the safe knowledge that the Germans, Italians and French had already done so.

These reservations apart, the British government has had very few problems with the details of the 1992 programme covered in this volume. Indeed, in most cases it has been the member-state that is most keen to see progress. Britain can therefore claim, with some justification, that it is highly *communautaire* as regards the mainstream 1992 provisions. Restrictions on access to the British market have in any case been removed by national policies.

The challenge facing Britain

The challenge facing Britain is more fundamental than whether this or that item of national regulation will have to change. The British approach to market regulation rests on the interpretation of national public interest by Parliament, or, more accurately, by the government of the day. However, the only viable approach to European regulation precludes reliance on public-interest criteria, as is evident from the terms of the Treaties and subsequent secondary legislation, including the 1992 provisions. The exercise of national public interest must, of course, be constrained if a single market is to be created. But to substitute a European concept of public interest would require agreement by all the member-state governments as to what that means. Such agreement is unlikely, if not impossible. For the British, the logic of the 1992 process therefore implies accepting the establishment of a European regulatory framework that limits recourse to discretionary powers based on nationally defined public interest.

This fundamental issue has been largely concealed by the practical resemblance between British deregulation and the 1992 programme. In other areas of EC activity, such as fiscal harmonization or monetary union, in which the differences between British philosophy and EC proposals are immediately apparent, the conflict finds expression in a defence of British sovereignty. The regulatory framework that is being established by the 1992 process contains the elements of an economic constitution, which, once established, will not be readily amended or changed. Thus, in effect, the options for future British governments risk being curtailed by deregulatory agreements, which cannot be said to rest on a broad national consensus, but only on the preferences of the government in office. The Conservative government has found little difficulty in denying itself in practice the use of discretionary powers available under British statutes to promote national industrial-policy objectives. This would not necessarily be the case for any future Labour government. Future frictions between national policy and EC constraints cannot therefore be ruled out. A more negative national approach to 1992 could also emerge if a government of whatever political complexion finds its objectives frustrated by EC rules. Those member-states that can draw on a broad national consensus can also pursue their national objectives more consistently; and they are likely to have certain advantages when it comes to influencing European policy.

The 1992 process also has important implications for Britain in the field of social and employment policy. Under the Thatcher governments of the 1980s, deregulation embraced the labour market and thus undermined most forms of social contract, both explicit and implicit, at least at a national or sectoral level. Indeed, corporatism of this kind and its associated rigidities were seen as a major source of Britain's economic malaise during the 1970s. If there was to be any dialogue between the social partners, it was argued that this should take place at the level of the firm and be left to a voluntarist approach. The watchword of the 1980s was individual enterprise, not consensus. This theme was adopted and endorsed by management who wanted to be allowed to manage free from the ties of any negotiated social consensus. By the end of the 1980s, this view had became so entrenched that both the British government and the

British business community had difficulty in understanding or accepting that the German CDU or CSU, BDI or BDA, might still see a need to retain a consensus-based approach. It is therefore not surprising that the British Conservative government, supported by the CBI, should try to block the creation of a European Charter of Fundamental Social Rights, which was, after all, seeking to introduce at the EC level what in Britain had been removed at the national or sectoral level during the 1980s. Both government and business had, however, underestimated the continuing importance placed on social dialogue and social consensus in the other member-states.

British business support for the single market
British business views of 1992 have overall been positive. This is surprising given the persistently high trade deficit with the rest of the Community, especially with Germany, and the generally vulnerable position in which British industry finds itself at the beginning of the 1990s, despite the improvements of the past decade. At the time that interviews were carried out, there was still a belief in the rhetoric of British economic revival. Indeed, profitability was high and investment increased strongly towards the end of the 1980s. However, as our case-studies have shown, British companies do not in general figure highly among the key players in the single market.

Another reason for business support for the single market is that access to the British market has been granted unilaterally anyway, so British entrepreneurs might as well seek equivalent access to the rest of the EC market. Whether in the field of financial services, procurement or takeovers, access to the British market causes few major headaches for any company wishing to invest or bid for orders. There was no protection on offer for British companies, and the British business community had little alternative but to endorse the single market.

Like other national markets, the British market is no longer an adequate base from which to build global competitiveness. In most manufacturing sectors, the British market is considerably smaller than the German one. German unification will, in the long term, result in a further contrast in market size. British companies' need for access to the rest of the EC, in particular the German market, is greater than the need for German companies to gain better access to the British market.

Yet the case-studies in this volume raise doubts as to whether British companies have in practice risen to the challenge of 1992. In the sectors considered, local-market presence will still be an important element of success. In this sense, the skills and resources needed to make the most of the internal market differ little from traditional exporting strengths, in which German companies have over the years excelled. 1992 is no short cut. The question then becomes whether 1992, and the associated increase in awareness of the wider European market, is prompting British companies to channel more resources and expertise into their sales efforts in the rest of the EC. Interviews conducted with firms for this project (mostly during 1989) suggested that, although many had studied the impact of 1992, few had done much to establish a presence across the EC and even these had done so on a relatively small scale. This finding is confirmed by the surveys carried out during the same period by the Bank of England on financial services and by NEDO on manufacturing. Extensive DTI and CBI campaigns certainly helped to increase awareness of 1992, but the overall impression left after surveying the British corporate response is one of caution, marked by a reluctance to commit resources to any strategic objective of increasing market share in the single European market.

British companies are uniquely vulnerable to hostile takeovers in that, compared with the rest of the EC, the market for corporate control is truly open only in Britain. Yet when it comes to making a strategic acquisition in order to gain access to markets in other parts of the EC, British companies face some significant structural barriers. The British propensity to make and accept takeovers should be set in the context of what has been called short-termism within British business circles. Many manufacturers argue that the emphasis on short-term returns on investment in the City of London makes it harder for firms to compete internationally. A growing number of people in the service sector echo the point that they are therefore both vulnerable to foreign takeover and less able than their continental competitors to finance strategic acquisitions. Yet the financial institutions and the City Takeover Panel oppose any measure which might discourage this takeover activity, arguing that an open market for corporate control helps to ensure that British companies are well managed.[2] With business split down the middle, the government's liberal bias has been decisive, hence the continued British emphasis on maintaining an open market for corporate control. However, the decision in September 1990 to refer the joint bid by Thompson CSF and GEC for Ferranti to the MMC, because of the involvement of foreign public enterprise, shows that intervention in order to ensure a level playing-field may be considered legitimate.

Changing trade-union attitudes

British trade unionists have fundamentally rethought the tradition of voluntarism in labour relations as a result of their involvement in developments in the European Community. Increasingly, the Trades Union Congress (TUC) argues that European regulation provides an opportunity for progressive social and employment policies. This, together with the European Commission's commitments to dialogue with the social partners, has transformed attitudes towards the EC within the British labour movement. The TUC wholeheartedly supported the Social Charter of the EC, and accepted the need to modify its traditional voluntarist approach to industrial relations and labour law, although this will not be without such costs as the prohibition of pre-entry closed shops, which British unions have fought to defend from national deregulation.

How durable this change of attitude will prove remains to be seen. It has come mainly from the leadership and has still to filter through to the grass roots, i.e. the shop stewards and those trade unionists active in local Labour parties. The remaining ideological differences within the European trade unions, and a general lack of resources, also constrain transnational cooperation. Yet if there were a permanent shift towards European-wide involvement, or even European-wide collective bargaining, it would clearly have a long-term impact on the British political system.

The German approach

The German approach to market regulation emphasizes the establishment of a clear and consistent regulatory framework within which market forces can operate. In most cases this regulatory framework embodies policy objectives, agreed on the basis of a broad political and social consensus and often anchored in statutes. Once the overarching policy objectives have been established, day-to-day fine-tuning or regulation is delegated to independent bodies. The classic, and most well-known, example of this kind of *Ordnungspolitik* is the Bundesbank, but it also finds application in a range of other areas, such as competition policy that is administered by the independent Federal Cartel Office.

German *Ordnungspolitik*, essentially liberal in character, is based on the underlying principle that markets should be allowed to operate freely, but subject to regulation designed to satisfy agreed objectives. In the case of German monetary policy, the central objective is price stability; and in competition policy it is the maintenance of effective competition. The

101

approach is not interventionist in that day-to-day regulation is carried out by independent authorities, insulated from (short-term) political pressures. It is not, however, deregulatory in its thrust because it recognizes a legitimate function for the state in regulating markets.

The German response to 1992 has been, and continues to be, influenced by this national policy stance. In contrast to the situation in Britain, however, the German approach to market regulation has developed in parallel with the evolution of the Community. Indeed, both Germany and the EC have drawn on similar philosophies in order to deal with the issue of how to structure regulatory policy in a liberal economy that comprises a number of different states. From the outset, therefore, Germans have faced questions as to the consistency of their evolving national approach to regulation with what has been emerging at the EC level. Broadly, the Germans have interpreted emerging EC policy to be consistent with their *Ordnungspolitik*. Thus German opinion favours a central European bank, or Eurofed, based on the Bundesbank model, and opposes a system in which there would be direct day-to-day political control of monetary policy. To follow our other example, the FRG has also argued for an independent European Cartel Office to implement European competition policy.[3] Whereas in Britain an increase in EC competence has been opposed because of the loss of sovereignty involved, in Germany such a shift in competence is opposed if it grants the European authority discretionary powers that would undermine their *Ordnungspolitik*.

There is little support in Germany for any Anglo-American type of deregulation. This is borne out by the experience of Chancellor Helmut Kohl's government with its efforts to deregulate. On coming into power in 1986, and with the British experience of deregulation and privatization in mind, the Kohl government set up a Deregulation Commission to report on what measures should be taken to reduce what was widely seen outside Germany as the over-regulation of the German economy. The objective of setting up an independent Commission was to investigate sectors, such as insurance and transport, in which it was thought that there was over-regulation. Independent reports were produced that generally favoured liberalization, but consultations with interest groups created a storm of protest during 1989. Unlike the British government, which has been able to force through deregulation measures without consulting interest groups, the Kohl government was not prepared to attempt to change the agreed regulation without seeking a political consensus. The embedded antipathy towards deregulation has meant that the work of the Deregulation Commission has had to be treated with political kid gloves in order to avoid political unpopularity.

It is still too early to say what effect, if any, the unification of Germany will have on this deregulation initiative. On the one hand, it could put a premium on continuity, given that the five new Länder have to catch up with the rest of the Federal Republic. The new Länder will have to shift from a heavily regulated economy, with predominantly publicly owned industry, to a more mixed and more open economy. To leap straight to full liberalization could be asking too much. Also, West German companies could well resist deregulatory change being piled on top of pressures to invest in the five new Länder. On the other hand, there may be cases, such as telecommunications (see Chapter 5), in which the need to move quickly may result in change that will tend to undermine the established consensus in the Federal Republic.

The challenge facing Germany
In contrast to the British, who over the past decade have often led the efforts to liberalize within the EC, the Germans have tended to be either in the mainstream of EC member-states or erring towards the less deregulatory end of the spectrum. In a number of key areas, German policy has moved closely in parallel with the evolution of Community policy. For example, the liberalization of German telecommunications was interwoven with the evolution of Community policy, each repeatedly drawing on the same thinking. The insurance industry provides another example of close linkage between the liberalization in German rules and EC policy. In this sector there was both domestic and wider European pressure for liberalization. The German insurance industry, as Chapter 6 shows, is one of the most regulated in the EC. The 1992 initiative led to a debate about liberalization, and in particular about whether the introduction of EC legislation should not be used as a means of wide-scale liberalization of the sector, going beyond that required by the EC. After much debate, it was decided to go only as far as the EC legislation required at the time.

Wherever the established German regulatory framework diverged from what was proposed for the EC, the German government tended to resist change, despite pressure from various sources. There is therefore a clear sense in which Germany was forced to change as a result of 1992. Thus, in contrast to the leadership role taken by the British in some key areas of the 1992 programme, the Germans have tended to be followers. This is shown in most of the case-studies covered in the previous chapters. It is true with regard to financial services and telecommunications, although once Germany had liberalized the latter, it moved a lot further than most other EC member-states. There was a rearguard action against tougher EC rules in public procurement, and in the standards sector there was resistance to EC directives that were seen to be diluting the existing German standards.

The German consensus

As will be clear already, many aspects of the German approach to market regulation spring from the emphasis on consensus. The depth and political significance of the German commitment to social and political consensus is not well understood in Britain. It is seen as a major objective by the government and the social partners alike, and by the major political parties as the basis for the stability of the Federal German system. Unification is likely to result in even greater efforts to build and retain consensus. The social partners argue that consensus has been the basis for the consistent strength of German economic performance, in that it reflects an implicit social contract in which labour recognizes the need for stable and long-term economic growth in return for a share in future wealth. Although unification was brought about by a Treaty on the Creation of a Monetary, Economic and Social Union,[4] the economic problems facing the five new Länder pose a major challenge. The level of financial support from the old FRG suggests, however, that the consensual approach will ultimately prevail in the larger Federal Republic of Germany.

The consensual approach is reflected in both public policy and corporate approaches to the single market. At the national level, members of the Coalition government, led by the Ministry of Labour and Social Affairs, have argued that it is unacceptable to have 286 items of EC legislation aimed at creating a single market for business, and nothing on the social dimension. The German government has therefore been one of the strongest supporters of legally binding social measures to implement the European Social Charter. The importance that the government attaches to consensus is well illustrated by the series of nationwide 'Europe conferences' (Europa Konferenzen) held during 1989, with participation by all leading interest groups. At these, members of the government explained and discussed the likely impact of the single market on the Federal Republic – for the precise purpose of establishing a national consensus on the 1992 process. This contrasts with the British exercises, which were primarily informative and aimed at making business aware of the opportunities created by 1992.

Industrialists, employers and trade-union leaders, in the shape of the BDI, BDA and DGB, have sat down and sought to find agreed positions on the single market. The results have taken the form of a number of joint declarations on European issues, beginning in July 1989 with a joint statement on the single market. Although the agreements are necessarily based on lowest common denominators, the fact that both sides felt a dialogue was necessary reflects the commitment to retain the national consensus in the face of the changes being brought about by 1992. The most immediate challenge took the form of the debate about the viability of the Federal Republic as a location for investment, the so-called *Standort* (location) debate. This was initiated in May 1987 by the BDI's efforts to use 1992 as a lever to reduce employment costs in order to prevent what it saw as the danger of investment flowing out of the FRG to lower cost areas of the Community. After prolonged discussion, the view that emerged by the middle of 1989 was that higher productivity, stemming from a better-trained workforce and good infrastructure, would enable the Federal Republic to compete as a location for invest-ment. Indeed, although average labour costs in Germany are consider-ably higher than those in Britain – and were so even before the rise in British wages brought about by inflation at the end of the decade (2,008 ecus against 1,417 ecus in 1984) – unit labour costs have been within the middle EC range throughout the 1980s.[5] The open question is how the location debate will be affected by unification. The five new Länder could clearly offer a relatively low-cost location for investment, at least in the short term, but they lack the infrastructure and to some extent the human capital that enabled the old Federal Republic to remain competitive.

The German social partners have sought to defend the national con-sensus against challenges from the 1992 programme, with the trade unions naturally to the fore. German employers' associations have been happy to use 1992 as a means of strengthening their national negotiating position. The BDI and BDA therefore go along with the tough anti-social-dimension line adopted by UNICE under the leadership of the CBI. This has led many British industrialists to conclude that their German counterparts would be delighted if the single market would undermine the German domestic consensus. But when this consensus is under challenge, the overwhelming reflex is to protect it because it has proved to be a source of strength and stability in the past.

Consensus extends down to company level and finds its statutory expression in *Mitbestimmung* (shared management), which provides em-ployees with places on the supervisory boards of companies. These representatives sit together with other stake-holders in a company, such as the bankers, and thus maintain an implicit social contract at company level. This in turn fosters a sense of commitment to the long-term growth of the company. Change of ownership as a means of bringing about change in corporate control signifies the end of the social contract and is thus seen as unwelcome.[6] This affects the relationship between the companies' financial stakeholders and the management, as well as that between management and employees. In many cases there is also a form of implicit contract between companies and the local communities in which they operate. The local town or state will, for example, provide vocational training in return for a commitment to the community on the part of the company. It is therefore widely held that hostile takeover bids are destructive and should not be made easier by EC provisions that, for example, lower the barriers to takeover (see Chapter 2). This identification with the company is an important influence on the German thinking about corporate adjustments to the 1992 process. This is not to be confused with protectionism in the normal sense; the German approach to 1992 is much influenced by a concern to minimize changes that challenge established and successful patterns of behaviour. To put it simply, the German model is seen to be successful and there is no great incentive for change.

German industry's emphasis on continuity

What goes for the German regulatory framework holds equally for German company views about 1992. The German market is in many cases considerably larger than the British market and offers a sound base from which to develop European and global strategies; German industrialists have therefore got much more to lose than their British counterparts. Although German companies agree that a single market is needed in order to end the fragmentation of European markets, which hinders the competitiveness of European industry, their greater strength means that they also have a greater stake in the status quo. German companies are prepared to consider change, provided it is orderly.

This preference for orderly change does not mean that the German economy is rigid, as was often claimed during the early part of the 1980s. It can be readily found in industries in which oligopolistic market structures have existed for some time, such as in the power-plant and telecommunications sectors. All companies interviewed supported the creation of a single European market, but the underlying assumption was that this would take the form of a European oligopoly in which they would play a leading role. The desire for orderly change is most clearly visible in manufacturing, in which the emphasis appears to be on a continuation of organic growth. Managers in manufacturing companies stressed that their competitors in Europe, and particularly their French competitors, were jumping into acquisitions and strategic alliances without sufficient thought. In the service sector, German companies, such as the Deutsche Bank, Allianz and a growing string of regional banks, have been much more aggressive, and have recognized that effective access to local markets requires a local presence and thus probably the acquisition of an established company. The regional banks now realize that they must develop national and European, if not international, strengths if they are to compete. As a result, there has been a greater use of intra-EC acquisitions or strategic alliances by German financial-services companies than by manufacturing companies.

Interestingly, many German industrialists expressed support for the creation of a single market, both for commercial reasons relating to the interests of their own company and because of its contribution to European integration. This political dimension to 1992 was largely absent in interviews with British managers, many of whose views echoed those of the more sceptical members of the Conservative government as to the merits of European political integration. This may also reflect the more corporatist German approach, in which business sees its pursuit of economic efficiency as at the same time fulfilling political and social functions. A similar response is evident in the West German approach to German unification. The effort to bring about a successful unification of Germany is being carried by every sector of society, including West German managers and trade unionists.

Trade unions defending the status quo
German trade unions regard the 1992 process as threatening to lower the level of social provision. This reflects the generally higher levels of wages and employment conditions in the FRG compared with those in Britain. Thus, whereas the British trade unions showed considerable enthusiasm for the European Social Charter, the German unions were rather critical of it because it threatened to undermine German levels of social provision by creating a floor below German standards. Nevertheless, the German trade-union movement supports the social dimension to the single market, in that it is likely to help raise levels of social provision and working and safety provisions in the rest of the EC. There is no question of unions accepting a lowering of German standards in order to

match the level of EC provisions, but they recognize that there are limits to the degree of divergence that can exist. In interviews conducted during 1989, the general view was that 1992 imposed limits on further progress towards improved national conditions, unless the level of working conditions could be improved elsewhere in the EC in parallel with 1992.

German trade unions generally support the established *Ordnungspolitik* in the FRG. For example, they do not favour the use of merger-control policy as an instrument of industrial policy, but believe that the Federal Cartel Office should defend effective competition. The commitment to consensus varies among unions and among the Deutsche Gewerkschaftsbund (DGB) and individual unions. Some of the industry unions, such as IG Metal, place more emphasis on the exercise of trade-union power than the DGB does, and do not believe that joint statements between the DGB and BDI or DBA have much value.

German trade unions see themselves as being in the forefront of efforts to establish a genuine European collective-bargaining procedure. IG Metal has, for example, promoted the use of trans-European works councils along the lines of those established under German law on plant level representation. Cross-border works councils were indeed established in three companies: Thomsen, Bull and Gillete. Ideally, the German unions would like to see these kinds of arrangements set up in many more companies, and they see the ideological standpoints of the trade unions in other member-states as an inhibiting factor. For their part, the other trade unions, including – at least until recently – the British TUC, have seen the German unions as being much too close to management or too corporatist.

There remains, however, a strong commitment to strengthen cooperation between the trade-union movements in the various member-states, in order both to create a more effective lobby in Brussels and to move ahead with EC-wide collective bargaining. The DGB believes that the European TUC is becoming more effective, and that there are now greater resources available for trade unions at the EC level.

Germany therefore faces a major challenge when it comes to the details of the 1992 programme. Its overall approach to market regulation is sufficiently similar to the emerging EC approach to accommodate marginal change at the macro level without too much difficulty. This also implies that Germans will work hard to ensure that their practices of consultation and consensus are adopted at the European level. It must therefore be expected that there will be powerful resistance to wholesale deregulation.

Interest representation

How do these differences affect the ways in which groups in the two countries seek to influence policymaking at the national and EC levels? If 1992 changes the regulatory environment, the ability of companies, industries or member-state governments as sponsors of national industrial interests to influence this environment can be of considerable importance. Before discussing the British and German lobbying efforts, two general points should be made. First, our case-studies showed that in order to influence the shape of legislation in the critical early phases, representatives of the various bodies concerned need to master the detail of the policy brief and to know how it affects the industries concerned. The Commission officials working on a draft directive are open to constructive, positive proposals and often actively welcome the opportunity to discuss alternative approaches with experts who know how the sector concerned operates. To have a real impact, however, these experts must have the ability to build coalitions across the EC. This is true for the member-states, but also for interest groups, such as UNICE, the European TUC or a sectoral trade organization at the EC level. The Commission must get a qualified majority in favour of any directive, and representations from one national interest group are easily fended off by reference to divergent views within the same sector in other member-states. The ability to establish and maintain contacts with the Commission and national officials, know the characteristics of the industry, and build coalitions with equivalent organizations across the EC, requires considerable resources. Interviews carried out during this research project showed that there are few people at any time in the Community who are capable of mastering such a brief. Indeed, in each of the member-states there are perhaps only a handful, in the case of some technical standards even one person.

The second general point flows from the first. There was little evidence to suggest that Britain's generally negative position on broader EC issues had any immediate impact on the technical level of representation. At the later stages of policy formulation, when political influence rather than mastery of a brief are the determining factors, the political isolation of Britain on Community issues in general may have been more significant. But at the level it really counts, namely, the formative stage of EC legislation, the key factors are expertise and the level of resources devoted.

If the British and German business lobbies are compared, one is struck by how remote the representative bodies had become from policy formulation and influence by the end of the 1980s as a result of the British government's aversion to anything approaching consensus politics. British ministers have not felt obliged to consult and have done so only when they chose to. Indeed, paradoxically, industrial and employers' organizations were less influential under the Conservative governments of the 1980s than under the previous Labour government. Sometimes they learned of major policy decisions from the press. For example, in May 1988, the CBI learned of the government's plans to restructure the DTI, the sponsoring ministry of business, only a few days before they were announced. Such an absence of dialogue between the principal national industrial federation and its main sponsoring ministry would be inconceivable in Germany.

Companies in both Britain and Germany choose the most suitable channel for representation. For example, on some issues, such as the Social Charter, British companies have sought to work with the British government and against EC proposals. On other issues, British firms have worked with the Commission or European-level industrial confederations and against the national government, as in their support for the European merger-control regulation at the time that the British government was maintaining a resolute reserve on the issue.

By comparison with their German counterparts, British entrepreneurs operate from a poorly resourced base when they seek to influence EC legislation. This is important given that effective representation, and above all proactive representation aimed at influencing the shape of the Commission's proposals, requires considerable resources. In this regard, the non-corporatist ethic of Britain in the 1980s militated against channelling resources into influencing regulatory policy.

Interviews with British and German interest groups showed that, where the German BDI would typically have one or two full-time professionals working on a particular directive, the British CBI would have perhaps one-half or one-third of a general administrator. Compared with their German counterparts, British sectoral trade associations and trade unions are fragmented, often poorly resourced and with widely varying levels of expertise of EC affairs, ranging from very high to non-existent. This partly reflects the British voluntarist approach: membership of trade associations being voluntary in the United Kingdom, but obligatory in Germany. For example, the CBI represents about 200,000 companies, and the BDI 1.2m, which is reflected in the resources available for representation.[7] In addition, trade unions have been weakened by the effects of the Conservative government's policies on the economy and employment legislation during the 1980s.

This under-representation of British interests on EC (as indeed on national) policy issues should not, however, be construed to mean that British industrialists do not influence policy. On the contrary, particular companies or individual business leaders have often been close to the policy process. The critical variable has been not the structures of formal dialogues but the access of favoured individuals to the upper echelons of the government. The committees set up by the DTI for the 1992 awareness campaign consisted of favoured friends, not representative organs. Similar informal links are much more difficult to set up at the European level; moreover, the European organs are less susceptible to regulatory capture of this nature.

Finally, the general decline of British industry has, of course, weakened the voice of British industry in Europe. In the competition among rules that is taking place in the process of the 1992 programme, the poor performance of the British economy, and particularly British industry, hardly helps to sell the British approach. There is a tendency, which came out clearly from our interviews with German industrialists, to judge the British approach on its results. German industrialists would politely point out that on these terms there was little reason to shift from the German to the British approach on, say, the regulation of corporate takeovers. Given these handicaps, it is remarkable that the British business lobbies have managed to achieve as much as they have.

The prospects for convergence

Our analysis of the German and British approaches to 1992 shows a tantalizing mix of congruence and contrasts. It suggests that the EC process contains much of the spirit of the British deregulatory approach, but embodies practices often more familiar in Germany. Thus we come to the question of whether convergence of British and German policy and practice is probable or not.

The chapter on mergers and acquisitions reveals two different pictures. Within the EC, it is possible to identify a continued process of policy convergence on competition policy. In the case of takeovers, however, there are few signs of a convergence between the British open market for corporate control and the more closed German model. The agreement on merger policy represented a significant step towards policy integration. From now on, large-scale mergers will be dealt with by the EC and not by the national authorities. This agreement emerged precisely because there was convergence between all member-states.

For Britain the decision meant no apparent change of policy, because the Conservative government had been pursuing for some time a competition-based merger policy, as opposed to industrial policy. However, some change is implied in the sense that British policy is now so anchored in EC legislation that the scope for the national exercise of discretionary power will be limited. This builds on the considerable degree of convergence that has already taken place in policy on restrictive practices in the member-states. For their part, the Germans have had to accept that some degree of discretion at the EC level is needed in order to ensure that the regulation can be used effectively. On balance, however, the final shape of the regulation turned out to be closer to the German approach.

As for takeovers, our evidence suggests little significant convergence (see Chapter 2). The British open market for corporate control is a peculiarity in the Community, in stark contrast to the German system, in which change of ownership plays a relatively small role in corporate adjustment, and hostile bids are seen as unwelcome. German industrialists who were interviewed saw no benefit in moving towards a more open market for corporate control. There is some market-led pressure for change in the German financial community, which sees the development of a larger and more open market for shares as necessary if Frankfurt is to compete with Paris and London as financial centres, but the majority of German firms, not to mention trade unions, would oppose such a move. Policy-led changes in the shape of EC directives harmonizing regulation of takeovers and company law in the EC will not remove the structural and cultural differences that exist. There is therefore little chance of much convergence, and so it seems unlikely that a single market for corporate control will be created.

In public procurement it is still too early to say whether there will be convergence. The key question is whether the national characteristics of supply are weakened by 1992 and purchasing practices changed. Up to now, 1992 has clearly accelerated the demise of the national champion, especially on the British side, where national policies have also resulted in recent liberalization. But purchasing practice has still to change. The case-study on utilities with national networks showed that changes on the purchasing side may have to await more radical liberalization through, for example, agreement on competitive common-carriage measures across the Community. In this respect, British and German approaches are likely to diverge, with Britain being more prepared to accept a deregulation of the utilities.

On technical standards and certification there has been convergence. If anything the Germans have had to give more ground. The new approach to standard-making and mutual recognition was more in line with the British deregulatory approach. The new-approach directives did force a number of changes in national policy, even in areas previously regarded as sacred cows. For example, the machinery-safety directive was fiercely opposed by the German Ministry of Labour and Social Affairs because it was seen to be weaker than the national standards. On the other hand, the 1992 process resulted in a need to improve the British standard-making procedures in order to ensure that the interests of British companies were reflected in the standards that were produced.

There has been convergence in the field of telecommunications, with the Germans tending to give ground in bringing their national regulation in line with the emerging EC policy. This is one area in which deregulation in Britain has provided a lead for the rest of the Community. Opponents of liberalization, especially in Germany up to 1985, argued that liberalization would result in chaos and inefficiency. But the British experience showed that it was possible to liberalize without chaos. The EC regulatory framework that is now emerging represents a balance between the more liberal and the more restrictive member-states. It also reflects the desire of all member-states, including Britain, to retain regulatory control of the basic network. There is as yet no single market in telecommunications networks. They retain their national monopolistic positions, with each network benefiting from considerable monopoly rents. Real liberalization would open up national network monopolies but would require regulatory control to be transferred to the EC level. No member-state is prepared at present to accept this. In this sense telecommunications is an example of a sector in which the EC provides a means of retaining regulatory control by setting limits to competition within the EC. But there has been important convergence, and the changes in the FRG as a result of moving towards a common EC framework have been more far-reaching.

In financial services, market-led factors are bringing about liberalization and thus a move towards the British model. This represents a major challenge for the Germans, especially in insurance. Our case-studies in financial services suggest that here, as in other fields, the German regulatory system will respond by adopting certain elements of British practice while rejecting others. In this sense, the follower can benefit from the lessons of the leader. By gearing liberalization in the EC to the adjustment of German companies, the competitive advantage gained by the

113

British suppliers of financial services can be held in check while the German restructuring takes place.

Conclusion

In short, our case-studies suggest that there are signs of convergence, resulting from both market-led and policy-led factors, between the British and the German approaches to regulatory regimes. These are not major shifts, but, given the semi-permanent nature of EC regulatory systems, such shifts as do occur have important implications for integration, since they are unlikely to be reversed. Convergence is not necessarily the destination. It is possible to conceive of competition among rules continuing indefinitely. Indeed, this course may be favoured, as a means of ensuring plurality, by both national governments and regulators who do not wish to lose sovereignty. The British support for competing currencies is one of the more obvious cases in point.

In general, the 1992 process means the creation of a regulatory framework that limits the ability of national governments to use discretionary powers to intervene in the economy, but does not provide the basis for significant Community-level discretionary intervention.

The concept of a regulatory framework that limits the discretionary powers of governments (and parliaments) is far removed from British traditions and, on balance, the overall approach to regulation in the single market is likely to be closer to the German approach than to the traditional British one – not because of German domination but because it has proved the most effective. Thus, although the Germans will have to sacrifice some of their regulatory policies, Britain faces the more fundamental change from a public-interest/discretion-based approach to one that is closer to the German *Ordnungspolitik*. The voluntarist approach of the British to labour relations, and their love of non-statutory self-regulation, is also under threat as the structure of regulatory regimes in the EC becomes more formalized.

Thus it can be argued that the use of a kind of *Ordnungspolitik* at the Community level will not necessarily result in a zero-sum game between national and EC regulators; rather, it will clarify the division of authority between them, and will limit the ability of national governments to use discretionary powers as a means of obstructing the creation of a single market. 1992 deregulates by limiting national regulation. Regulation at the Community level can therefore be seen as a necessary part of the process of ensuring liberalization and making a reality of the single European market.

NOTES

Chapter 1

1 For a general debate on the economic impact of the 1992 programme, see Alexander Italianer, '1992 Hype or Hope: a review', paper prepared for the LINK meeting, Paris, August 1989. mimeo.

2 Commission of the European Communities, *Completing the Internal Market*, COM(85)310, Brussels, June 1985.

3 See for example, Jacques Pelkmans and Alan Winters, *Europe's Domestic Market*, Chatham House Paper, RIIA/RKP, London, 1988.

4 Reference to speech given by Mrs Margaret Thatcher at opening ceremony of 39th Academic year of the College of Europe, Bruges, 20 September 1988.

5 *Reve-Zentral AG v Bundesmonopolverwaltung für Branntwein*, Case 120/78, 1979, ECR 649.

Chapter 2

1 Merger-control provisions had already been included in the 1951 Treaty of Paris, which established the European Coal and Steel Community.

2 Proposal for a Regulation (EEC) of the Council on the control of concentrations between undertakings', *Official Journal of the European Communities*, C92/1, 31 October 1973.

3 For detailed analysis of the differences, see *Barriers to Takeover in the European Communities*, Coopers and Lybrand for the Department of Trade and Industry, London, 1989.

4 See for example, Competition *Policy in the OECD Countries*, OECD, Paris, 1989, p. 7.

5 See *Barriers to Takeover*. These figures most probably inflate the British takeovers and underestimate the German takeovers because they are based on reported M&As, and information on British M&A activity is much more comprehensive than that on German activity.

6 On this point, see *Barriers to Takeover*.

7 See 'Proposal for a Council directive on the control of concentration between undertakings', *Official Journal* C234/5, 17 December 1986.

8 See Jürgen Lindemann, 'Antitrust Problems in Mergers and Acquisitions', paper presented to the CEPS conference, 30 January 1990.

9 See statement by Dr Ernst Niederleithinger, Vice-President of the Federal Cartel Office, in *Frankfurter Allgemeiner Zeitung*, 11 August 1988.

10 See *Amended proposal for a Council Regulation (EEC) on the control of concentrations between undertakings*, COM(88)734 final, 19 December 1988.

11 See Article 1 of 'Council Regulation on the control of concentrations between undertakings', *Official Journal*, L395, 30 December 1989.

12 See *Frankfurter Allgemeiner Zeitung*, 21 December 1989.

13 See for example, Peter Montagnon (ed.), *European Competition Policy*, Chatham House Paper, RIIA/Pinter, London, 1990.

14 For more detail on this issue, see Stephen Woolcock, *European Mergers: National or Community Control?*, RIIA Discussion Paper no. 15, RIIA, London, 1989.

15 For a discussion of this, see Stephen Woolcock, *Corporate Governance in the Single European Market*, RIIA Discussion Paper no. 32, RIIA, London, 1990.

16 *Proposal for a Thirteenth Directive on Company Law concerning takeover and other general bids*, COM(88)823, 12 December 1988.

17 This was completed in November 1989, see *Agence Europe*, 27 November 1989. Although British approval of the merger-control regulation was not explicitly linked to the Commission doing more work on takeover barriers, there was an implicit link.

18 See Communication from the Commission to the Council, 'Obstacles to takeover and other general bids', *Europe Documents*, 15 May 1990.

19 See Jonathan Charkham, *Corporate Governance and the Market for the Control of Companies*, Bank of England Panel Paper no. 25, Bank of England, London, March 1989.

Chapter 3

1 See Commission of the European Communities, *Research on the 'cost of non-Europe': volume 5 - Public Procurement*, Commission of the European Communities, Brussels, 1988, p. 18.

2 Ibid. A straight comparison of import ratios gives a very inaccurate

picture. A major contractor on a project will sub-contract or buy components from suppliers in other member-states. This trade does not appear in import ratios, which are based on the contract with the main supplier.

3 See 'Rapport du groupe stratégie industrielle; travaux publics', in *Research on the 'cost of non-Europe': volume 5.*

4 See Francis McGowan and Steve Thomas, 'Restructuring in the Heavy Electrical Industry: the Effects of the Single European Market', Science Policy Research Unit, University of Sussex, 1989. mimeo.

5 In 1986, US firms won contracts for public works in the EC to the value of 6bn ecus, whereas contracts won by EC firms in other markets were worth a total of 600m ecus. See *Rapport du groupe stratégie.*

6 See Communication from the Commission to the Council on *An action programme for public procurement in the Community*, COM(86)375. There are in fact likely to be seven directives, since there will be two compliance directives and two services directives.

7 For a discussion of the social and regional dimension of public procurement, see Communication from the Commission to the Council, *Public Procurement: Regional and Social Aspects*, COM(89)400 final, 24 July 1989.

8 For early drafts of what were originally the two directives covering energy, water and transport, as well as telecommunications, see *Bulletin of the European Communities*, supplement 6/88 'Public procurement in the excluded sectors'. This also contains the supporting Communication from the Commission.

9 See for example, Trades Union Congress, 'Maximizing the benefits, minimizing the costs', *TUC Report on Europe 1992*, London, 1988; For the European Parliament's proposals on the procurement procedures of entities providing water, energy and transport services, see *Report for the Economic and Monetary Policy Committee*, Delorozoy, PE 128.101 final, 6 April 1989.

10 See 'Council Directive on the coordination of the laws, regulations and administrative provisions relating to the application of review procedures to the award of public supply and public works contracts', COM(89)665, in *Official Journal*, L395, 30 December 1989.

11 See House of Lords Select Committee on the European Communities, *Compliance with Public Procurement Directives*, session 1987-8, April 1988.

12 See *Proposal for a Council Directive coordinating the laws, regulations and administrative provisions relating to the application of Community rules on the procurement procedures of entities in the water, energy, transport and telecommunications sectors*, COM(90)297, July 1990.

Chapter 4

1   *Official Journal*, L109, 26 April 1983.
2   See Communication by the Commission on *Instruments for the Realization of the Internal Market*, COM(89)422, Annex VI, 7 September 1989.
3   On this point, see, for example, J. Pelkmans, 'The New Approach to Technical Harmonization and Standardization', in *Journal of Common Market Studies*, March 1987.
4   See *Offical Journal*, C10, 16 January 1990.
5   Currently there are three programming committees in CEN (for machinery, building products and gas appliances) and three in CENELEC and ITSTC, a joint CEN/CENELEC/ETSI steering committee for the field of information technology.

Chapter 5

1   Werner Neu, Karl-Heinz Neumann & Thomas Schnoering, 'Trade patterns, industry structure and industrial policy in telecommunications', in *Telecommunications Policy*, March 1987, pp. 31-44.
2   H. Ungerer and N. Costello, *Telecommunications in Europe*, European Perspectives Series, Commission of the European Communities, Brussels, 1988, pp. 32-3.
3   Ibid., pp. 113-4.
4   *The Economist*, 25 February 1989.
5   Peter F. Cowhey, 'Telecommmunications', in Gary C. Hufbauer (ed.), *Europe 1992: An American Perspective*, Brookings Institution, Washington DC, 1990, p. 177.
6   *Panorama of EC Industry*, Commission of the European Communities, Brussels, 1989, pp. 12-18.
7   *Communications Week International*, 1 October 1990, p. 15.
8   *The Financial Times*, 14 November 1990.
9   *Reform of the Postal and Telecommunications System in the Federal Republic of Germany: Concept of the Federal Government for the Restructuring of the Telecommunications Market*, R. V. Decker's Verlag, Heidelberg, 1988, pp. 6ff.
10 Ibid., p. 68.
11 *The Financial Times*, 21 November 1990; *Communications Week International*, 17 September 1990, p. 6.
12 European Communities Green Paper on *The Development of the Common Market for Telecommunications Services and Equipment*, 1987, p. 181; *Italian Republic v Commission of the European Communities*, Case 41/83, 20 March 1985.
13 COM(88)901 final, 16 May 1988.
14 *Communications Week International*, 11 December 1989, pp. 1-2; *PC*

Business World, 17 July 1990, p. 4.

15 *Communications Week International*, 3 September 1990, pp. C2-C3.

16 *The Financial Times*, 11 July 1988; Deodato Gagliardi, 'Standards in European Telecommunication', paper presented at the Financial Times Conference on World Communication, London, 13 December 1988.

Chapter 6

1 Paolo Cecchini, *The European Challenge 1992: Benefits of a Single Market*, Wildwood House, Aldershot, 1988, pp. 37-42.

2 Commission of the European Communities, *Research on the 'cost of Non-Europe': volume 9 - Financial Services*, Commission of the European Communities, Brussels, 1988, pp. 139-79.

3 Ibid., p. 76.

4 'Coordination of regulations on insider trading', Directive 89/592, in *Official Journal*, L334, 18 November 1989.

5 *European Report*, 28 July 1989; *The Financial Times*, 20 and 21 June 1989, 16 and 19 December 1989.

6 British Bankers' Association, *The Second Banking Directive: a Commentary*, British Bankers' Association, London, March 1988, p. 7.

7 *The Financial Times*, 21 June 1989; British Bankers' Association, *Article 7 of the EC Commission's Proposal for a Second Banking Directive: 'Reciprocity'*, British Bankers' Association, London, 17 May 1989.

8 Xavier Vives, *Banking Competition and European Integration*, Centre for Economic Policy Research, London, 1990.

9 Confederation of British Industry, *Preparing for 1992: EC Liberalization of Financial Services and Insurance*, Brief no. 18, February 1989, p. 1.

10 Bank of England, *The Single European Market: Survey of the UK Financial Services Industry*, Bank of England, London, May 1989.

11 Ibid., pp. 14-15.

12 Ibid., p.17.

13 Ibid., pp. 15-25.

14 Matthew Crabbe, 'EC Law Shapes the Pattern of European Banking', in *Euromoney*, June 1989, p. 64.

15 *The Financial Times*, 22 August 1989.

16 *The Financial Times*, 21 March 1989.

17 *The Financial Times*, 20 July 1989.

18 *The Financial Times*, 4 March 1988.

19 See Dieter Farny, 'Erwartungen europäischer Versicherer an den Binnenmarkt', in *Zeitschrift für die gesamte Versicherungswissenschaft*, vol. 1/2 1989, p. 100.

20 'Seventh Report of the Monopoly Commission, 1986/7', *Bundestagsdrucksache*, no. 11/2677, 19 July 1988, pp. 233-80.

21 Figures supplied by the Association of German Insurers.
22 *Commission of the European Communities v Federal Republic of Germany*, Case 205/84, 4 December 1986.
23 'Second Council Directive 88/357/EEC of 22 June 1988 on the coordination of laws, regulations and administrative provisions relating to direct insurance other than life assurance and laying down provisions to facilitate the effective exercise of freedom to provide services and amending Directive 73/239/EEC', in *Official Journal*, L172, 4 July 1988.
24 See, 'Recommendation of the Bundestag of 17 November 1989', in *Bundestagsdrucksache*, no. 11/5735, 20 November 1989.
25 *Handelsblatt*, 16/17 March 1990, p. 1.
26 See 'Comment on the freedom to provide services in the non-life sector', in *Gesamtverband der Deutschen Versicherungswirtschaft*, June 1988.
27 'Proposal for a Council Regulation (EEC) on the application of Article 85(3) of the Treaty to contain catagories of agreements, decisions and concentrated practices in the insurance sector', COM(89)641 final, 18 December 1989, in *Official Journal*, C16, 23 January 1990.

Chapter 7

1 Between 1986 and 1988 the Federal Republic of Germany provided, on average, 1,134 ecus per worker in manufacturing compared with 723 ecus per worker in British manufacturing. See Joseph Gilchrist and David Deacon, 'Curbing subsidies', in *European Competition Policy*.
2 See *Corporate Governance in the Single European Market*.
3 See for example, Heinrich Hölzler, 'Merger control', in *European Competition Policy*.
4 See *Bulletin der Presse-und Informationsamt der Bundesregierung*, no. 63/ S. 517, Bonn, 18 May 1990.
5 The higher social provisions in Germany which German trade unions are seeking to defend against 'social dumping' within the EC are reflected in the higher non-wage labour costs, an additional 70% of wage costs in the Federal Republic against 40% in Britain. See 'Antwort der Bundesregierung auf die Grosse Anfrage der Koalition zum Socialraum Europäische Gemeinschaft', *Bundestagesdrucksachen*, no. 11/4700, June 1989.
6 Dr Colin Meyer, 'Capital Markets and Corporate Governance: A European Comparison', Centre for European Policy Research, London, 1989. mimeo.
7 See for example, 'Antwort der Bundesregierung'.